D0617493

# Assessing Service-Learning and Civic Engagement

## PRINCIPLES AND TECHNIQUES

# Assessing Service-Learning and Civic Engagement

## PRINCIPLES AND TECHNIQUES

Sherril B. Gelmon, Dr.P.H.

Barbara A. Holland, Ph.D.

Amy Driscoll, Ed.D.

Amy Spring, M.P.A.

Seanna Kerrigan, M.Ed.

**Campus Compact**

**Campus Compact**

**The Mission of Campus Compact**

Campus Compact is a national coalition of college and university presidents
committed to the civic purposes of higher education. To support this civic
mission, Campus Compact promotes community service that develops students'
citizenship skills and values, encourages collaborative partnerships between
campuses and communities, and assists faculty who seek to integrate public
and community engagement into their teaching and research.

Funding for this publication is provided by the Corporation for National and
Community Service.

**Campus Compact**
Brown University
Box 1975
Providence, RI 02912
phone: (401) 867-3950
email: campus@compact.org
website: www.compact.org

Copyright © 2001 Campus Compact.
All rights reserved.

No part of this book may be reproduced or transmitted in any forms by any
means, electronic, mechanical, photocopying, recording, or otherwise, without
the prior written permission of the publisher. For information on obtaining
reprints or excerpts, contact Campus Compact, campus@compact.org.

ISBN: 0-9667371-7-2

# Table of Contents

# List of Tables

# Preface

*S*ervice-learning is an educational methodology which combines community service with explicit academic learning objectives, preparation for community work, and deliberate reflection. Students participating in service learning provide direct and indirect community service as part of their academic coursework, learn about and reflect upon the community context in which service is provided, and develop an understanding of the connection between the service and their academic work. These learning experiences are designed through a collaboration of the community and the institution or academic unit/program, relying upon partnerships meant to be of mutual benefit. Improvement and sustainability of the experiences and the partnerships are enhanced through formal assessment activities that involve community, faculty, student and institutional voices and perspectives. This handbook presents a set of well-tested strategies for assessing the impact of service-learning and similar programs.

## The Evolution of this Assessment Monograph

This monograph emerged from our various projects, first at Portland State University (PSU) and then from other institutions and national research initiatives. Our goal was to develop an assessment model that responds to the complexity of service-learning and other strategies for civic engagement in higher education. As we began model development, it became clear that we needed to address multiple constituencies simultaneously in order to truly understand impact. In the context of higher education, these constituencies were identified as students, faculty, community, and institution. When we began, a literature review informed us that there was little help available already in the literature in terms of models, approaches and instruments, so we decided to use a case study method for testing multiple assessment strategies that would be useful to both our service-learning and other community service activities at our institution.

We started our work in 1995, and soon began presenting our conceptual model in various venues. We immediately received many requests for copies of our assessment methods, and therefore decided to prepare a handbook that could be widely available. We published a first edition of this handbook in June 1997 through the Center for Academic Excellence at Portland State University (Driscoll, Gelmon, et al., 1997). That edition was based on development of a large number of different assessment instruments, and our experiences pilot-testing those instruments in ten service-learning courses at PSU. We quickly learned from our analysis of those results that we could make refinements in the conceptual matrices that guided our assessment activities, and that many of the instruments could benefit from further refinement. These refinements were made, and a second edition was published, again by PSU, in April 1998 (Driscoll, Gelmon, et al., 1998). The second edition, in particular, has been warmly received by academics and community partners interested in techniques and sample tools for use in service-learning assessment.

Over the past several years, we have presented multiple workshops at various national, regional and local meetings on assessment, relying upon the workbook as a reference and an ongoing resource. Well over 2,000 copies have been printed and distributed nationally and internationally through PSU. Because of our commitment to the advancement of service-learning and civic engagement assessment strategies, we have always sought to make this assessment model and associated tools widely available for use.

## The Current Edition

This expanded edition is motivated by two main factors. First, the authors have continued to work with this conceptual material in various projects at multiple higher education institutions and with multiple community organizations. We have continued to learn about its use, and are compelled to share our insights into background, supporting literature, advantages and limitations, and practical guidance on use of the various instruments. Our understanding of the utility of this set of strategies as an adaptable approach for assessing engagement activities in addition to service-learning has expanded through various national projects. There is now much more to explore about the strategies and their potential applications for assessing various civic engagement endeavors.

Second, in recent years there have been increasing calls for an electronic version of the handbook to facilitate access to the material and minimize the preparation time necessary to use the instrumentation. We have wanted to respond to these calls in order to facilitate the distribution of the materials and easy access to the various instruments.

The current edition, while grounded in the earlier PSU versions, offers a much broader perspective on assessment strategies. We are therefore grateful to national Campus Compact for providing us with the support, made possible by the Corporation for National Service, to prepare this new edition and to facilitate its production.

## Focus on Service-Learning

The primary focus of our assessment efforts has been on curricular service-learning. In each section, we also provide illustrations of other applications of this material, such as in other kinds of experiential education, co-curricular activities, institutional change processes, partnerships, or other kinds of faculty development initiatives. While we recognize that there are many potential applications of this material, and encourage such use, nonetheless the primary focus and therefore most of the illustrations relate to service-learning. Hopefully this handbook can be a helpful resource in these other contexts as well.

As described in the overview of assessment principles and strategies, this handbook is also intended as a resource for assessment for continuous improvement, not just for demonstrating outcomes. Thus the reader will find that improvement methods and concepts are woven throughout the narrative, the approaches, and the instrumentation itself.

This handbook is not intended to be the ultimate guide to service-learning. For resource materials on service-learning, the reader is referred in particular to Campus Compact's *Introduction to Service-Learning Toolkit* (Campus Compact, 2000) which provides a comprehensive overview of service-learning and civic engagement, and includes valuable resources and bibliographies.

## Organization of the Handbook

The handbook is presented in three main sections. The first is an overview of assessment philosophy and methods. While many resources exist on assessment, we have included an overview of assessment strategies in this edition of the handbook as a resource for framing our approach to assessment. As well, this section will ensure that users of this handbook have ready access to basic information about assessment.

The second section presents each of the four assessment constituencies in a separate chapter (students, faculty, community, and institution). Each of these chapters includes:

- a brief review of the literature,

- discussion of issues in assessing impact on that constituency,

- the assessment matrix,

- strategies for assessment of that particular constituency (including advantages and limitations of particular instruments), and

- examples of assessment instruments we have used in various settings.

Each instrument is introduced by a discussion of purpose, preparation, administration, and analysis, specific to that instrument.

The final section focuses on using the methods and analysis of data. Again, we offer best practices and suggestions for use based on our collective experiences. This section incorporates discussion on strategies for making assessment work.

## Conclusions

We have learned that the act of assessment is important for its role in communicating the value of service-learning to many audiences. Developing a "culture of evidence" (Ramaley, 1996) to describe and document the impact of service-learning supports its institutionalization, facilitates the ability of course-based learning to be translated into scholarship, and fosters trust and communication among the various involved constituencies. Engagement in the act of assessment is a valued element of the service-learning experience for each constituent group as it articulates its unique perspective and learns from and appreciates the perspectives of the other constituent groups. Assessment is valuable beyond measurement of outcomes, and warrants our investment of time, our expenditure of resources, and our commitment.

## Acknowledgements

This work has been supported over the years by a number of institutions, funders, and partners. We are grateful to the dozens of institutions, and individuals at those institutions, who have participated in various projects to test and improve this assessment model; they are too many to name! The following list recognizes the major supporters; any omissions from this list are unintentional.

### Institutions

- Portland State University

- California State University, Monterey Bay

- Northern Kentucky University

### Funders

- The Corporation for National Service

- The Pew Charitable Trusts

- Bureau of Health Professions, Health Resources and Services Administration, U.S. Public Health Service

- Fund for the Improvement of Post-secondary Education, U.S. Department of Education

- National Fund for Medical Education

- W.K. Kellogg Foundation

- David and Lucille Packard Foundation

### Partners

- Campus Compact

- Center for Academic Excellence, Portland State University

- Center for the Health Professions, University of California San Francisco

- Community-Campus Partnerships for Health

- Community Care Network Demonstration Program, Hospital Research and Educational Trust, American Hospital Association

- Council of Independent Colleges

- Health Professions Schools in Service to the Nation

- Healthy Communities of the Columbia-Willamette, Inc.

- Institute for Healthcare Improvement, Interdisciplinary Professional Education Collaborative

- Institute for Nonprofit Management, Portland State University

- Many participating students, community partners, faculty and institutional representatives

*Sherril Gelmon, Amy Spring, Seanna Kerrigan;* Portland State University
*Barbara Holland;* Indiana University Purdue University at Indianapolis
*Amy Driscoll;* California State University, Monterey Bay

June 2001

# Assessment Principles and Strategies: An Overview[1]

*I*nstitutions committed to civic engagement and service-learning must be able to demonstrate the impact of these initiatives to ensure quality for student and community participants, to justify resource investments, and to inform the improvement and expansion of such programs. Understanding and articulating "impact" requires knowledge and expertise in the design and application of assessment methods.

This handbook provides basic information on practical methods and tools for assessment planning, design, and implementation. The material can be used for a campus-wide service-learning initiative, for individual courses, or for other activities related to civic engagement and community involvement. Since, throughout the text, the primary focus is on developing a comprehensive assessment strategy on the institutional or programmatic level, the word "program" occurs often. Nevertheless, as has just been noted, these materials can also be adapted for individual faculty use in freestanding courses.

## Context for Assessment

Increasingly, higher education is experiencing a shift away from a traditional emphasis on teaching to a new emphasis on learning. Barr and Tagg (1995) have described this as a movement from seeing colleges as institutions whose function it is to provide instruction to seeing them as institutions designed to produce learning. If one thinks of the core concepts that attend teaching and learning — for example, knowledge, focus, the curriculum, instruction, design strategies, student roles, and organizational change — a framework such as Table 1 can be used to illustrate the transition from the "old" to the "new." Note that service-learning and other forms of community-based education all demonstrate characteristics of the new — emphasizing the application of knowledge, a team and community focus for learning, collective instruction and collective curriculum definition, an integrated sequencing of courses, and active student learning. These concerns are all important to keep in mind as one begins to consider how one can best assess the impact of such programs.

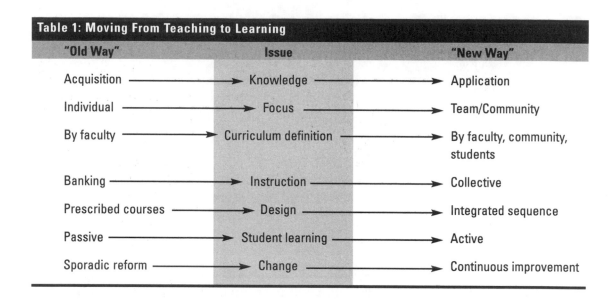

| Table 1: Moving From Teaching to Learning | | |
|---|---|---|
| **"Old Way"** | **Issue** | **"New Way"** |
| Acquisition | Knowledge | Application |
| Individual | Focus | Team/Community |
| By faculty | Curriculum definition | By faculty, community, students |
| Banking | Instruction | Collective |
| Prescribed courses | Design | Integrated sequence |
| Passive | Student learning | Active |
| Sporadic reform | Change | Continuous improvement |

The language of "civic engagement" and community participation is increasingly evident in discussions of trends in higher education. Ehrlich (2000, p. vi) describes civic engagement as "working to make a difference in the civic life of our communities." Such an enterprise changes the function of the institution, creates new challenges for faculty roles, offers opportunities for new collaborations with community partners, and affects not only what students learn but also what should be taught. These changes inevitably lead to questions such as "what impact is engagement having on the institution and its component parts?" To answer questions like this one, carefully constructed assessments must be created — assessments that ask clear questions, collect appropriate data, and analyze and report results in a meaningful way.

## Why Do Assessments?

Why do we do assessments? Many say that universities have to prepare better-educated students; therefore, the primary reason for assessments is to improve student learning. Others believe that a key reason to conduct assessments is to provide immediate feedback to enable program leaders to make incremental changes, responding to identified needs and concerns. Over the long term, assessment data can provide the basis for program planning and for redesign and substantive improvement.

Why is assessment currently so important? Across the United States, there is an increasing interest in assessment due to regulatory requirements, public demands for educational accountability, and administrative concerns about resource utilization — not to mention the growing interest in assessment for program improvement (Gelmon, 1997). With ever-increasing calls for accountability from funding agencies and accreditors, particularly with regard to resource accountability, there exists a regular demand for clear assessment data.

At the same time, many campuses find it difficult to articulate how a service-learning program should be assessed, let alone how the results of such an assessment can contribute to an understanding of civic engagement. But as we learn more about the institutional impact of a commitment to engagement, the main reason for documenting that impact reveals itself as essential to ensuring sustained, high quality relationships among all participants. Faculty, students, community partners and institutional participants all come to a partnership with different concerns and expectations; these demand a complex and intentional assessment strategy (Holland, 2001). Furthermore, although interest in service-learning and engagement continues to grow, some faculty remain cool to these new endeavours and remain sceptical, demanding strong evidence for the value of this work. Assessment can produce the evidence of impact many faculty require and, thus, can lead to broader participation.

## Service-Learning and the Engaged Campus

As institutions explore and discuss the concept of an "engaged campus," some faculty demand to know what exactly engagement is in relation to academic work and whether such a focus represents a true descriptor or key trait of their institution's missions and actions. What does an engaged campus look like? How does it result in different faculty work and expectations? What are the characteristics of engaged students and the nature of their learning experiences? What can be observed about community-campus partnerships? All of these questions can begin to frame a campus-based assessment of engagement.

Since studies show that an institutional commitment to engagement is strongly linked to the inclusion of community-based learning experiences in an institution's curricula (Holland, 2001), service-learning can be viewed as an instructional strategy appropriate for increasing civic engagement (Hollander & Hartley, 2000; Gelmon, 2000a). This monograph is intended to help fill a void in the published literature about assessing the impact of service-learning across a broad range of constituencies.

Engagement and partnerships represent a new dimension of academic work. The multidimensional nature of partnerships and engagement is reflected in several recent publications. For example, the 1999 report of the Kellogg Commission on the Future of State and Land Grant Universities, *The Engaged Institution,* offers a set of characteristics that form a seven-part "test" of engagement (Kellogg Commission, 1999):

- **Responsiveness:** are we really listening to the communities we serve?

- **Respect for partners:** do we genuinely respect the skills and capacities of our partners in collaborative projects?

- **Academic neutrality:** do partnerships maintain the university in the role of neutral facilitator despite the existence of potentially contentious issues?

- **Accessibility:** is our expertise equally accessible to all the constituencies of concern within our communities?

- **Integration:** does the institutional climate offer new opportunities for integrating institutional scholarship with the service and teaching missions of the university?

- **Coordination:** are academic units, institutional support offices, and groups of faculty, staff, and students dealing with others productively and sharing/translating their knowledge into something the public can appreciate?

- **Resource partnerships:** are resources committed to the task sufficient?

Each of these characteristics offers a potential focus for planning and assessment. Similarly, the *1999 Presidents' Declaration on the Civic Responsibility of Higher Education* (Campus Compact, 1999) includes the "Campus Assessment of Civic Responsibility," which provides a framework for institutions to conduct a baseline self-assessment of their readiness for civic engagement by involving administrators, trustees, faculty, staff, students, alumni, and community partners in a deliberative process of describing institutional commitment and conditions. The questions included in the Compact's assessment framework address topics such as leadership, curriculum, involvement in community public policy development, campus and faculty culture, diversity, community-campus partnerships, communication, and community improvement.

Analogously, Holland (1997) has created a matrix of key organizational factors that can guide campus explorations of commitment to engagement based on the degree to which engagement is seen as an element of campus mission. For each level of commitment, the matrix provides measures and features associated with successful and sustained engagement programs.

Furco (2000) has developed still another guide for assessing the institutionalization of service-learning. He proposes five dimensions for such an assessment: 1) philosophy and mission of service-learning, 2) faculty support/involvement in service-learning, 3) student support/involvement in service-learning, 4) community participation and partnerships, and 5) institutional support. Multiple categories are then articulated for each dimension. A team involved in self-assessment would consider each criterion and determine its school's place according to three levels of institutionalization: 1) critical mass building, 2) quality building, and 3) sustained institutionalization.

The "engaged campus" is also being discussed in many higher education forums, and one of the key areas that emerges here as vital for any assessment effort is an analysis of community-university partnerships. Such partnerships are an essential component of engagement and form the basis for service-learning activities. A review of lessons learned through projects related to service-learning and other forms of community-based learning (Holland & Gelmon, 1998) suggests that some of the key areas in need of assessment include the nature of relevant partnerships; understanding the needs and assets of both the educational institution and the community; defining community; leadership roles; curricular placement and emphasis; the nature of learning; and partnership sustainability.

## Beginning the Assessment Process

Assessment serves a useful purpose as a mechanism to tell the story of what one has learned from one's work — articulating that learning for oneself as well as for others. In beginning any assessment process, one should ask a series of key questions. The answers to these questions will frame the design of the assessment process:

- What is the aim of the assessment?

- Who wants or needs the assessment information?

- What resources are available to support the assessment?

- Who will conduct the assessment?

- How can one ensure the results are used?

These questions are important for a number of reasons. Every assessment process should have an aim and stated purpose. Without them, there may seem to be little reason to carry forward the required work. Furthermore, the person or agency wanting or needing the assessment may dictate the nature of the actual work to be carried out — is it mandated by a funder, is it part of an accreditation or other regulatory review, is it part of an individual's personal performance review? To ensure implementation and follow-through, an assessment plan must identify the resources that will support the assessment and the person or persons who will do the work.

Too often, assessments are designed without a clear understanding of their resource implications, with frustration resulting from the fact that the plans drawn up do not correspond to the realities of available resources and expertise. Finally, it is important to be able to ensure that the results of an assessment process will be attended to and used. Designing and conducting a comprehensive program assessment, only to see the results of that process ignored, can leave those involved with a deep sense of futility.

As suggested above, assessment is important, first, to articulate what has been learned for oneself. Many professionals in higher education today have little time to stop, reflect, and consider the impact of their work. Articulating the implications of that work can help to delineate issues, describe strategies, and highlight areas where further work is needed. Assessment can also provide an opportunity to stop and celebrate successes that have been achieved — something rarely done. Finally, assessment can help us to focus our thinking in ways that result in new insights and identify opportunities for improvement.

Second, assessment helps us to articulate our learning for others. It can facilitate our sharing lessons we have learned and can transmit knowledge essential to others' learning. In particular, a strategic assessment plan can identify factors of import to others conducting similar or parallel work.

Finally, we should note that assessment can vary in its scope depending upon its constituencies and purpose. In the context of an institutional review for regional accreditation, an assessment plan might be university-wide. On the other hand, a department or program might undertake assessment for internal review purposes, for professional review (by a state governmental entity or a specialized/professional accreditor), or as one aspect of a departmental/program plan. Campus-wide general education programs are often the focus of assessment efforts aimed at gaining greater understanding of how such programs affect multiple student populations. New service-learning initiatives are often the focus of intensive assessment efforts as institutional leaders seek to determine the comparative value and expense of service-learning as compared with other pedagogical approaches. Since assessment of service-learning and civic engagement demands that one understand multiple areas of impact, this handbook presents detailed discussions of how one can understand their impact on students, faculty, community partners, and the institution as a whole.

## Who Should Be Involved in Assessment?

Successful assessment requires bringing together players central to the activity being assessed, and helping them to step outside their normal roles and to create a new culture — one that facilitates pooling their collective interests to focus on the program, service, department, or other activity being assessed. For this reason, assessment can have a transformational impact on the unit or activity in question (Magruder et al., 1997).

In the context of service-learning assessment, multiple players are essential to provide a broad perspective on program impact. Students, faculty, community partners, and institutional leaders all have a distinctive role to play as key informants. In addition, faculty may be involved in the design and administration of assessment activities related directly to their classes. Community partners may wish to play a similar role in the design and administration of assessment procedures related to their responsibilities. Graduate students may also represent a valuable resource in helping with assessment design, administration, and analysis, for such work may have bearing on their own programs of study. Finally, institutional centers for teaching and learning, community outreach, institutional research and assessment, and/or service-learning can play important roles in various aspects of the assessment process.

Considerable debate exists regarding the merits of centralized versus decentralized responsibility for assessment. In some institutions, a central office has been developed to provide a focus within the institution's administrative structure and to serve as a campus-wide resource (see, for example, Palomba, 1997). While establishment of such an office is often viewed as evidence of an institution's commitment to assessment, one liability of such an approach is that faculty and/or departments may come to view assessment as solely the responsibility of that office, and as something about which they need not be concerned. Furthermore, results may be viewed with suspicion, since they derive not from the faculty but from a central administrative structure. One way to avoid problems like these could involve using a central office merely as the resource that supports, encourages, and facilitates faculty and/or departmental activities by encouraging, for example, buy-in to institution-wide assessment activities and by disseminating assessment results. Such buy-in is invariably enhanced by investing in faculty and staff development of assessment skills and by involving as many people as is feasible in the assessment process.

## Common Themes and Concerns in Beginning Assessment

Several concerns frequently arise at the beginning of the assessment process. One has to do with identifying appropriate and affordable expertise. At academic institutions, despite the presence of a number of disciplines where one might expect to find assessment expertise, one often can find few if any individuals who have the particular expertise needed to design, lead, and manage this work. At some institutions such expertise may indeed be found, but the individuals who possess it may already be over-committed to other projects and/or scholarly activities. If obtaining the necessary expertise represents a financial investment, it will be especially important to determine accurately what resources are available to support that investment.

A second concern relates to conceptualizing the focus of the assessment process; i.e., what precisely is to be assessed? When? For whom and for what purposes? The key questions identified in an earlier section can help to answer these questions and to frame the project, but considerable discussion may be needed to reach agreement on how best to frame the assessment plan.

Once the focus of the assessment has been conceptualized, another concern has to do with implementation — who is responsible? What resources do they have? What leverage exists to encourage people to participate in assessment activities and to co-operate in meeting data needs in a timely manner?

Still another concern relates to the selection of assessment methods. Those selected must take into account the purpose of the assessment and anticipated uses of the information collected as well as the potential burden the assessment activities will impose. When plans and needs are clearly set out and agreed upon, agreement upon methods may exist. However, it is not unusual to find participants who feel they themselves are the experts who should dictate specific assessment methods, particularly for use in their own classroom. In this regard, one especially common source of contention involves the ongoing debate between qualitative and quantitative data — a debate that includes questions of appropriateness, validity of results, generalizability, and other challenges. These questions, in turn, lead to discussions of rigor, specification of methodological needs, and ultimately to design issues that may go well beyond the resources available to support the assessment process.

A final concern revolves around the uses of assessment findings. Once again, problems can sometimes be avoided if there is discussion and agreement from early on as to what will be done with the data. Perceptions of a "closed" process or one intended to justify program closure or termination of faculty/staff positions will compromise the assessment process. Measures designed to guarantee an open process with agreed upon uses of the data obtained will assist greatly in facilitating assessment activities.

However, even a well-designed plan and emphatically open process may still encounter resistance — whether the threat the findings represent is real or perceived. If outside experts are brought in (either to provide an alternative to or to supplement internal experts), these outsiders may be intrinsically intimidating (the fear of airing "dirty laundry" in public). Sceptics will then question the rigor of the assessment plan and its methods, and may not be willing to accept that compromises in "scientific method" are sometimes necessary to meet deadlines. Other issues that may be raised include training to develop the internal capacity to conduct and manage the various components of the assessment as well as questions related to supervision, data collection, confidentiality, and data management. Finally, resistance is almost a certainty when the environment is already politically charged; for example, where there exists fierce competition for resources assessment data may help decide allocations.

While each assessment situation is unique, there nevertheless exist several responses that may help to overcome any resistance. Agreement upon the purposes of the assessment, public sharing of these purposes and careful adherence to the assessment's purposes and scope will help to establish the authenticity and legitimacy of the effort. Energy should also be deliberately invested in building buy-in for its value. Confidentiality of the respondents must be assured. Roles and tasks must be defined early in the process, and mechanisms for regular reporting, sharing of findings, updates, and airing of concerns must be clearly established.

## Assessment as an Improvement Strategy

Assessment can be viewed as a strategy for improvement — an integrated set of activities designed to identify strengths and areas for improvement, and capable of providing evidence to support future program planning. Assessment can be a useful mechanism to tell a program's story, but becomes most useful only when it is viewed as a value-added, routine undertaking — not as a burdensome add-on or species of "busy work." Assessment gives program managers, administrators, and other leaders a mechanism to identify what they have learned that is useful — both to articulate it internally and to share it with others.

Such an approach to assessment builds upon the "Model for Improvement" (Langley, Nolan, et al., 1998) that has been used widely throughout many sectors including higher education and health care. The core assumption here is that work/situations can usually be improved upon — or conversely that one needs to develop evidence to know that change is not needed. This model consists of three basic elements:

- **Statement of the aim:** "What are we trying to accomplish?" This clarifies the purpose of the assessment and makes it explicit to all those participating.

- **Clarification of current knowledge:** "How will we know that a change is an improvement, or if no change is needed?" This sets out what is known, and what the new knowledge will make possible once the assessment has been completed.

- **Testing of various improvements:** "What changes can be tried that will result in improvement?" Based on what has been learned, this will help to define what might be implemented as initial improvement strategies.

When one applies this model to higher education, the following questions help frame the assessment process (Gelmon, Holland, Shinnamon, & Morris, 1998; Gelmon, White, et al., 2000):

- **How is learning conducted** (e.g., service-learning or learning grounded in community-university partnerships)?

- **How does this pedagogical method become part of the curriculum** (how is it introduced, how is it developed, how is it integrated)?

- **How can this educational method be improved?**

- **How do individuals using this method know that a change is an improvement** (e.g., what comparisons can be made using pre- and post-data)?

In thinking of assessment as an improvement effort, one can focus on delineating issues that otherwise might not be obvious; describing strategies for future replication; highlighting areas for further work; and/or focusing thinking. Sharing the results of this effort through internal communications and/or through broader external dissemination via presentations at professional meetings, publications in professional literature, and postings on websites will also facilitate others' learning.

Using such an approach to assessment may well result in the identification of many opportunities for improvement. For example, curricular strengths may be clarified, validating existing knowledge and providing data to support the continuation of current activities. Or, conversely, deficiencies may be uncovered, thus providing the evidence and justification needed for making changes. Assessment may also serve to identify areas where faculty resources should be reallocated, and where faculty should be recognized for excellence or assisted in correcting deficiencies. In an institutional context, such activities are vital in order to consider broader issues of resource allocation (human, fiscal, physical, information, technological, and other resources), to inform public relations and marketing strategies, and to consider possible changes or realignments in organizational relationships and strategies.

## A Multi-Constituency Approach to Assessment

Over the past five years, the authors have developed a multi-constituency approach to assessment — initially, for use in assessing service-learning and now for use in a wider range of community-based learning situations. This approach began at Portland State University as part of an explicit effort to assess the impact of service-learning on students, faculty, the institution, and the community (Driscoll, Holland, et al., 1996). At that time, considerable effort was being invested in developing undergraduate and graduate service-learning courses, as well as in community-university partnerships, and the institution needed to understand the impact of these efforts. At this time, the university was also implementing a new general education program, and was attempting to create opportunities for service-learning experiences throughout that program, particularly in community-based senior capstone courses.

This approach was then greatly expanded and revised to assess the impact of service-learning in health professions education for the Health Professions Schools in Service to the Nation (HPSISN) program, a national service-learning demonstration program (Gelmon, Holland & Shinnamon, 1998; Gelmon, Holland, Shinnamon & Morris, 1998; Gelmon, Holland, Seifer, et al., 1998). This expansion added community partnerships as a fifth area of assessment focus. In both the PSU and HPSISN cases, the goal of the assessment effort was to explore implementation of service-learning and its differential impact on various constituencies, and to identify lessons learned for future service-learning programming. The HPSISN project was one of the first efforts to study the disciplinary implications of service-learning.

Subsequently, the model has been applied in other attempts to assess the impact of learning in the community. In two of these projects, students, faculty, and community partners worked together on community health improvement as part of their academic course-based work. These were:

- **An assessment of the Community-Based Quality Improvement** in Education for the Health Professions (CBQIE-HP) program where interdisciplinary teams of health professions students worked on specific community health improvement projects using the Model for Improvement methodology (Gelmon & Barnett, 1998; Gelmon, White, Carlson, & Norman, 2000), and

- **An evaluation of the Portland Tri-County Healthy Communities Initiative**, a cross-sectoral community development approach to building community collaborations to address specific community health problems (Gelmon, McBride, Hill, et al., 1998).

Another example of the adaptability of this approach to assessment design was demonstrated in 1998 when the goal-concept-indicator-method approach was used to create a matrix and methods for assessing the impact of a new Masters in Public Administration degree with a concentration in Tribal Administration, a program delivered to students using distance learning technology (administered from Portland State University, Mark O. Hatfield School of Government). This unique project, funded by a U.S. Department of Education FIPSE grant, called for an assessment model that tracked the effectiveness of program strategies and campus-tribal partnerships in meeting specific program goals and in creating satisfactory learning experiences for students in multiple locations (Holland, 2000a).

The design was adapted again in 1999 to create a unique assessment plan for a national project involving many types of civic engagement activities. The Council of Independent Colleges, funded by the W.K. Kellogg Foundation, awarded grants to eight private, urban liberal arts colleges to facilitate their exploration and implementation of an urban mission defined primarily in terms of civic engagement and partnerships. This effort resulted in interesting lessons about the unique challenges faced by smaller private colleges when they seek to enhance their civic engagement programs (Holland, 1999b; Holland, 2001).

All these projects have confirmed the utility of this multi-constituency approach for assessment of a broad array of partnership activities including but also transcending service-learning.

## The Assessment Matrix

The approach presented here is based on the development of a conceptual matrix, which is derived from project goals, that frames the assessment plan, guides the development of assessment instruments, and structures the data analysis and reporting. At PSU, it initially served as a framework to predict outcomes anticipated as a result of early anecdotal data available at that time. The approach was then refined, and began to be referred to as the "Goal-Concept-Indicator-Method" approach (Gelmon, Holland, & Shinnamon, 1998; Shinnamon, Gelmon, & Holland, 1999). It involves four primary questions:

- **What do we want to know?** This helps the evaluator to articulate the aim of the assessment, based upon the project goals.

- **What will we look for?** This leads the evaluator to identify core concepts that are derived from the project goals and the aim of the assessment.

- **What will we measure?** For each core concept, relevant measurable/observable indicators are specified which will enable the evaluator to measure or observe change or status.

- **How will we gather the evidence needed to demonstrate what we want to know?** At this stage, the evaluator identifies or develops appropriate methods and tools by which he/she can collect the information for each indicator, and identifies sources of the data.

Such an assessment framework thus provides a structure to guide evaluation; enables program administrators and evaluators to articulate clearly the framework for evaluation; and facilitates data collection, analysis, and reporting in a way that is true to the aims and goals of the assessment. In addition, this framework overcomes many of the sources of resistance to assessment previously described. It is illustrated in each of the following four sections in the context of a conceptual matrix for assessing impact on students, faculty, community and institution (see Tables 5, 6, 7, and 9). It strongly links assessment to program goals, and in this way increases the effectiveness of the assessment effort and the relevance of its findings.

The assessment framework is a tool that helps guide the thinking process in the design phase, serves as an important framework for implementation, and aids in defining and focusing the analysis. In its skeletal form, it appears as the matrix presented in Table 2. It has four main components: core concepts, key indicators, methods, and sources of information (Gelmon & Connell, 2000).

## Table 2: The Matrix Framework

| Core Concepts | Key Indicators | Methods | Source |
|---|---|---|---|
|  |  |  |  |
|  |  |  |  |
|  |  |  |  |
|  |  |  |  |

Core concepts are broad topic areas. To identify these, ask the question: 'What are the possible areas of impact that can be observed from courses, programs, or activities?" The definition of a concept is written in neutral language to provide a basic foundation for continued discussion and elaboration as to how the program may affect such a concept. Stating a concept in language such as "increase in _____" or "change in _____" introduces a bias into the assessment and compromises objective data collection. Refer to Tables 5-7 and 9 for examples of core concepts for each of the constituencies.

Key indicators are key evidence of impact, and are usually stated as the specific measurable or observable factors related to each core concept. To develop these, ask the question: "What might we look for to show that the concepts are being addressed?" What measures can we study to gain evidence of how the core concepts are being affected? As with the concepts, these should be stated in neutral rather than directional terms to avoid bias. There should be multiple key indicators for each core concept. Wherever possible, avoid defining indicators such as "number of," "increase in," "improved," etc., as this may limit the range of available data collection methods. For example, by stating "number of _____," one is directed to quantitative methods, whereas by avoiding this terminology one can use quantitative or qualitative methods. (Again, refer to Tables 5-7 and 9 for examples of suitable key indicators.)

Methods indicate the actual instrumentation or strategy to be used for gathering evidence through measurement or observation. In selecting appropriate methods, ask the question: "How will we look for it?" This refers to the instrument(s) one selects and, if applicable, to the way one will use it (them). The most commonly used instruments include:

- Surveys (self-administered or administered by another person)

- Interviews (in person or telephone)

- Focus groups

- Document reviews

- Observations

- Journals

- Critical incident reports

Each matrix in Tables 5-7 and 9 lists a variety of methods. A more detailed discussion of methods for each constituency is presented as those methods are introduced.

Sources of information may be a specific person, a group of people, a database, or a report. A source may be internal or external to an organization, and may be people who have had some personal contact or experience with the activity being assessed, or documentation containing relevant information.

In reality, different methods may be used for each indicator, and each source may provide data for many methods, but not all sources will be involved in each method, and not all methods will address each indicator. While there is a direct linear relationship between a concept and its related indicators, there is no such relationship between methods and sources.

## Using the Assessment Matrix

The completed matrix should be reviewed to ensure that the concepts are clear and distinct. Indicators should be verified to ensure that they are measurable or provide opportunities to collect evidence. If it is not possible to determine how an indicator will be measured or observed, it should be restated to enhance specificity. Program goals should be reviewed to ensure that the concepts and indicators reflect those goals, that all information included in the matrix is necessary to assess their accomplishment, and that no goal or major activity has been overlooked. Finally, it is important to ascertain that what has been set out for assessment is practical and feasible within the context of a specific organization; i.e., with reference to the resources available and the population(s) being served.

The matrix will be very useful in focusing the analysis of data. Key indicators of a program's success as listed on the matrix provide a critical point of reference that, although flexible, hold the evaluators accountable to the program's goals and objectives. Since the matrix will have been used in determining what information should be gathered and in developing the appropriate evaluation instruments, the data gathered should relate directly back to the key indicators and core concepts. In analyzing the data, one should focus on how the key indicators are reflected and to what extent they have been achieved.

## Issues in Instrument Selection

The key issue in selecting appropriate instruments is determining what will provide the best information to help accomplish the goals of the assessment. Selection of relevant assessment instruments involves evaluating their relative merits and determining which are best suited to specific needs (Gelmon & Connell, 2000[2]). Primary considerations in selecting specific instruments include:

- Design issues: time, expertise, resources available
- Data collection: ease, time, expertise needed
- Data analysis: skills needed, time, level of detail
- Response content: limited versus expansive
- Flexibility and accuracy of instrument
- Bias introduced by method
- Nature of questions: open-ended, closed-ended
- Side benefits or disadvantages

Each of these key considerations is illustrated in Table 3 for a variety of assessment methods.

Each assessment instrument also raises issues with respect to the trade-off between resources required to administer and analyze an instrument, and the value of the information that will be collected. Resources include money, equipment, expertise, and time for design, set-up, administration, analysis, and reporting. Key issues to consider in measuring the trade-off include:

- Set-up time
- Administration time
- Analysis time
- Other issues requiring resources (that may outweigh the potential value of the data)
- Nature of output

An approximation of the costs associated with each of these issues for each method is illustrated in Table 4. Again, in selecting instruments, one must determine what can be afforded that will provide the best information. Frequently, trade-offs of costs against potential data are necessary but ultimately do not compromise the overall quality of the assessment.

## Completing the Assessment Cycle

Once the necessary data has been collected, assessment leaders must be prepared to engage in extensive data analysis, synthesis, discussion, and report-writing. As mentioned previously, there are often lengthy debates on campuses about the relative merits of quantitative versus qualitative methods. Our own experiences show that a mixed methodology is most useful. Methods should be selected based on the kind of data that will be gathered as well as issues such as ease of data collection, ease of data analysis, and time and costs involved in both collection and analysis. However, consideration must also be given to the richness of the data that can be derived from various methods. Interviews, focus groups, observations, and reflective journals provide extensive and detailed information that necessitate a major time commitment to transcribe and analyze. In contrast, surveys provide less individual detail, but are relatively easy, inexpensive, and time-efficient to administer and analyze. Assessment leaders who do not have familiarity and expertise with various assessment methods should ensure they engage an expert to advise them during instrument development as well as data analysis. In each of the following sections, there appears information on the various assessment methods proposed, as well as the advantages and limitations of each.

A final step in the assessment process is reporting the results. A fairly typical method involves writing assessment report that describes 1) project goals, 2) what was done (programmatically), 3) what was measured, 4) the results, and 5) implications and/or recommendations. Reporting results should be guided explicitly by the matrix (using the concepts as major headings and the indicators as sub-headings); this will facilitate a synthesis of the findings and their presentation in a report. Assessment results can also form the basis for scholarly presentations and publications. However, care should be given to ensure that no confidential information is disclosed and that participants have given permission for the assessment findings to be released in a public forum.

Consideration should also be given to alternative forms of reporting to ensure wider and more rapid dissemination. For example, summaries of key findings can be presented in poster format and displayed in a campus cafeteria, at the library, student union, or other central location. Selected results and participant stories can be integrated into a university website. Other forms of reporting through annual reports, community updates, or focused brochures can also be used.

## Conclusion

Assessment provides a valuable mechanism for communicating the value of one's work. In particular, when seeking to document the effect of an approach such as service-learning or other activities demonstrating civic engagement, one must be able to provide evidence that the approach is making a difference — and be able to show the differential impact on various constituent groups. Good assessment requires collaboration and a commitment to invest time and energy. The very nature of assessment necessitates a long-term perspective, as the assessment effort is never complete. Nonetheless, continuous investment in the process provides the information needed to respond adequately to the assets and needs of those involved in a critical aspect of higher education reform and to seek continued improvement of the programs and services higher education provides.

The following sections identify the various "constituencies" relevant to the assessment of service-learning and related community engagement activities. Each section includes an overview, instruments, and guides to the use of appropriate instruments.

---

1 This text is adapted from "How Do We Know That Our Work Makes a Difference?" By Sherril B. Gelmon, published in *Metropolitan Universities* in Vol. 11, No. 2, fall 2000, p. 28–39. Permission granted by the editor.

2 This section is adapted from *Program Evaluation Principles and Practices: A Handbook for Northwest Health Foundation* (2000) by Sherril B. Gelmon and Amy Connell, with permission from the Northwest Health Foundation.

# Table 3: Comparison of Assessment Methods

| Instrument | Design Issues | Data Collection | Data Analysis | Response Content | Flexibility/Accuracy | Bias | Nature of Questions | Side Benefits/Disadvantages |
|---|---|---|---|---|---|---|---|---|
| **Survey** | Relatively complex and labor intensive; Requires expertise in survey design; Resources printing, mailing, responses | Effort to ensure participation; Sample or whole population; Use existing lists to recruit | Requires knowledge of statistics; Hand analysis or by computer | Limited; Must use simple words; Less detail | Accurate if questions valid; Little flexibility once designed | Little (controlled by question design) | Closed primarily | Generalizable if validated; Easy to report to different audiences; Results may be used for public relations and/or promotion |
| **In-Person Interview** | Relatively easy for expert to design; Sampling for subjects; Interviewer training | Selection of subjects important to ensure representation; Time intensive (one on one); Permission necessary | Lengthy; Need qualitative skills | Own words; Range of opinions; Detailed; Reflective | High flexibility within protocol; Use of probes | Potential for high interviewer introduced bias; Nonverbal issues | Open-ended; Conversational | Rich input; Comparability requires large number of interviewees; Labor intensive and time consuming |
| **Focus Group** | Relatively easy for expert to design; Selection of participants; Interviewer training | Ensure range of representatives; Time intensive; Expertise to facilitate; Agreement necessary | Lengthy; Need qualitative skills | Highly detailed; Dynamic | High flexibility within protocol | High potential to derail; Potential among participants; Nonverbal issues | Open-ended; Conversational | Participants can build upon each other and interact and therefore generate more ideas than an individual alone |
| **Telephone Interview** | Relatively easy for expert to design; Sampling for subjects; Interviewer training | Less time than in person; Potential for increased number of rejections | Lengthy; Need qualitative and quantitative skills | Own words; Range of opinions; Detailed | High flexibility within protocol | Eliminates nonverbal issues | Open-ended; Conversational or survey-type | High potential for early termination; Potential for fabrication of answers; Blend of strengths of surveys and interviews |

**Table 3: Comparison of Assessment Methods (cont.)**

| Instrument | Design Issues | Data Collection | Data Analysis | Response Content | Flexibility/Accuracy | Bias | Nature of Questions | Side Benefits/Disadvantages |
|---|---|---|---|---|---|---|---|---|
| **Observation** | Relatively easy for expert to design | Training of observers Time intensive to observe Permission necessary | Lengthy Need qualitative skills | Varied (fixed vs. open) Words of observer and quotes from participants | High flexibility | High because of observer Presence of observer may bias behavior | Open or closed | Can view "real" interactions Bias of observer's presence Opportunity for additional problem solving or consultation Augments primary data Generates lists of uncertain value |
| **Documentation** | Relatively easy for expert to design | Can be very time consuming to locate and review Initial access may take time Completeness, comparability and accuracy of records may be variable | Variable (depends on kinds of data collected) Analysis may already be available | Limited or extensive | Depends upon protocol and report style and format | Could be high from collection Bias of what is recorded | Open or closed | Augments primary data Could inspire improved record keeping Could raise issues not previously thought of Generate lots of information but of uncertain value |
| **Journals or Critical Incident Reports** | Relatively easy for expert to design | Highly dependent on willingness of participant to give the time | Lengthy if lots of content Analysis may already be available | Varies but should be detailed and in own words Highly personal | High flexibility | Respondent chooses to include or not include | Open within general guidelines | Augments primary data Reveal information not otherwise provided May generate lots of information with little context for evaluation |

**Table 4: General Guidelines on Time versus Value**

| Instrument | Setup Time | Administration Time | Analysis | Other Issues | Outputs |
|---|---|---|---|---|---|
| **Survey** | 1-4 days | Variable with survey length (5 minutes to one hour per survey) | Variable depending on question design and automated analysis | Need database and/or statistical expertise | Lots of data<br>Little measurable variation<br>Numerical reports<br>Generalizable in most cases |
| **Interview** | 1/2 day | 1.5 hours per interview | 3 hours per interview plus synthesis | Need qualitative data experience | Reams of paper/tapes<br>Individual stories<br>Personal words and anecdotes<br>Cannot quantify<br>Draw generalizations only after multiple interviews |
| **Focus Group** | 1/2 day | 1.5 hours per focus group | 3 hours per focus group plus synthesis | Need qualitative data experience | Reams of paper/tapes<br>Individual stories and words<br>Dynamic interactions within group<br>Peer dialogue<br>Cannot quantify<br>Can highlight new questions<br>Generalizable with sufficient replication |
| **Observation** | 1/2 day | As long as it takes to observe | Can be very lengthy or very brief | Time to observe<br>Access | Thin data<br>Useful to back up other sources and provide additional insights |
| **Documentation** | Time to get access | Lengthy | Lengthy | Access | Richness depends on quality<br>Complements narrative or numerical data<br>Capitalize on existing information |
| **Critical Incident or Journal** | 1-2 hours | Lots of individual time (not evaluator time) | Lengthy | Willingness of participants to give time and to respect the method or format | Rich stories, variable focus<br>Not generalizable<br>Promotes reflection<br>Backs up other methods/insights |

# Student Impact

## Why Assess the Impact of Service-Learning on Students?

The impetus for assessing the impact on students emerges from several constituencies. First, institutions of higher education are advocating for all courses to be rigorously assessed as institutions are constantly being held accountable for their graduates' level of preparedness upon entering the workforce. New programs and pedagogies such as service-learning must endure institutional examination to prove their value to the institution and their contribution toward student learning.

In addition to institutional demand for assessment, faculty members advocate for assessment in order to understand the impact of courses and pedagogies on student learning. Faculty who have a data-driven understanding of the impact of service-learning often utilize the data to continuously improve their teaching and the use of this pedagogy. Assessment also aids faculty who must demonstrate the rigor of this method of teaching among their colleagues.

Assessment provides a means for educators to respond to students' questions of "why?" they need to engage in this form of learning. Similar to the other constituents of service-learning, students seek to understand the effectiveness of service-learning as a component of their learning experience. As with the other constituents, the answer to these questions emerges from assessment data. Community members seek assessment data about students' learning and experiences in order to help them better understand how they contribute to the student learning activities. They may play an important role in evaluating the work of the students, and in understanding student development in terms of knowledge of community factors and social responsibility. Finally, service-learning practitioners advocate for assessment of impact in order to document the advantages and challenges of this work. Practitioners also utilize assessment data to document the innovative techniques faculty and students of various disciplinary backgrounds employ to achieve their student learning outcomes. Dissemination of these assessment results helps practitioners to improve the quality of student learning and contributes to the growth of the field of service-learning.

The need for and importance of increased assessment of service-learning was evidenced in 1991 when forty educational leaders were convened by the (then-named) National Society for Internships and Experiential Education at a Wingspread conference. Those involved in these initial discussions noted the growing number of students engaged in service each year (Giles et al., 1991). They identified lack of documentation of the students' experiences in service-learning courses. They found a paucity of data on the impact that this educational pedagogy had on students, and suggested that this was a national problem. These experts in the field felt that it was imperative to study specific areas of potential impact on students, including the following:

- What knowledge do students gain from participating in service-learning?

- Does service-learning affect students' perception of self and others?

- Does service-learning promote pro-social attitudes and behaviors?

- Does service-learning influence the development of effective citizens?

- How do factors of age, socioeconomic status, developmental stage, and background of students affect the outcomes of service-learning?

Conference participants encouraged colleagues across the nation to join with practitioners and students to conduct research in this field and to disseminate the findings. Since the Wingspread conference the urgency and importance of student assessment has increased as institutions of higher education place an increasing number of students in the community and sometimes do so without fully understanding the impact that this pedagogy has on student learning. To ensure quality of service and the best possible outcomes for learning, student service-learning experiences must be assessed systematically.

## Understanding the Impact of Service-Learning on Students

Since the 1991 Wingspread conference, researchers have worked to document the impact service-learning has on students (Alt & Medrich, 1994; Anderson, 1998; Astin & Sax, 1998; Eyler & Giles, 1999; Eyler, Giles & Gray, 1999; Gray, Ondaatje, et al., 1999). In Assessment for Excellence (1993), Astin presented a useful taxonomy that reflects the different types of college student outcomes assessed and the different forms of data collected. Student outcomes are described as either cognitive or affective. Examples of cognitive outcomes include theoretical knowledge and critical thinking, problem-solving, and decision-making skills. Affective outcomes include changes in attitudes toward community issues, populations served, community service, and personal values. The type of data collected is described as either psychological or behavioral. Psychological data refers to the internal state of the student, and behavioral data refers to the "student's observable activities" (p. 44). Finally, the time dimension of the study can focus on short-term (during college) or long-term (beyond college) time frames.

Most of the service-learning research to date has collected psychological data about student outcomes. Many of the studies measure a change either in students' attitudes towards others (Giles & Eyler, 1994; Myers-Lipton, 1996; Battistoni, 1997) or towards service itself (Buchanan, 1997; Gilbert, Holdt and Christophersen, 1998; Astin & Sax, 1998, Astin et. al., 2000). It is rare to find studies collecting data based on observable student actions. Battistoni's (1997) study included observations of student behaviors in the classroom, where principles of democracy were modeled. In addition, some studies ask students to report on their own behaviors. Astin and Sax (1998), Sax and Astin (1996), and Astin et al. (2000) include students' responses regarding their behavior while volunteering. While many of the studies are considered affective in nature (asking students to report on their attitudes), there is a growing body of literature focused on cognitive outcomes including critical thinking and decision-making skills (Wechsler & Fogel, 1995; Berson, 1998; Battistoni, 1997; Gilbert et al., 1998; Batchelder & Root, 1999).

Another methodological issue raised by Astin (1993) was the time dimension involved in each study. Most of the studies could be categorized as assessing short-term outcomes, or outcomes measured while the student is still in college. The study reported by Sax and Astin (1996) is the only one to collect data over time from students after graduation. Even within the short-term studies, researchers assessed students over different lengths of time. Jordan (1994) collected data from students engaged in a six-week service-learning experience and found suggestions that longer experiences may prove more productive. Substantial findings from Myers-Lipton (1996) and Astin et al. (2000) provide a rationale for studying the longer-term effects of service-learning on students.

These researchers have responded to the National Society for Experiential Education's call for research on service-learning (Giles et al., 1991). The Wingspread conference framed primary questions revolving around the issue of the impact this form of teaching and learning has on students. Since that time, researchers, practitioners, and doctoral students have attempted to bridge the gaps in the literature. The authors of this monograph have defined potential variables to be studied and suggested a mix of methods (Driscoll, Gelmon, et al., 1998). Others have used purely qualitative methods to study the students in their own service-learning courses (Battistoni, 1997; Gilbert et al., 1998). Universities such as the University of Utah (Buchanan, 1997) have gathered institution-wide data on the impact of service, while additional researchers have used larger national samples to gather quantitative data (Sax & Astin, 1996; Astin & Sax, 1998) on the effects of service.

In the special issue of the *Michigan Journal of Community Service Learning* on strategic directions for service-learning research, Eyler (2000) notes that most of the research of the past decade gives us adequate evidence of the impact service-learning has on student's personal and social development, yet there is little evidence of the cognitive impact this pedagogy has on student learning. The Portland State approach has provided the field with a set of research concepts and measurement strategies to mitigate this gap in the research (Driscoll, Holland, et al., 1996). The comprehensive set of techniques set forth in this monograph can be useful in assisting researchers with understanding and documenting student cognitive development documentation, as well as personal and social development.

Our assessment project began as a means to learn about and document the impact service-learning was having on students. To do this, we chose to employ a variety of different data gathering methods with the intent of determining the nature and variety of information each of the tools would uncover about the impact on students. As a result of testing various measurement methods, we now understand which strategies are most likely to aid us in documenting intellectual outcomes, problem-solving skills, and level of commitment among those students involved in service-learning.

## Assessment Matrix for Students

In the initial phase of our work at PSU we chose not to limit our investigation of possible areas of impact by having only one broad hypothesis. This was an exploratory study, and was comprehensive in its approach. Therefore, one of our original hypotheses was that service-learning would have an impact on students. We looked to the literature and early institutional observations to guide us in defining key concepts (variables) that would help us to understand the impact on students. The concepts are listed in Table 5. This list of concepts serves as the framework for defining focus and specific measurement for the assessment of the impact on students involved in service-learning. Once this list of concepts was identified, we identified measurable indicators for each concept that would demonstrate the presence (or absence) of the concept. Multiple indicators are needed for each concept in order to tease out the various ways in which students may experience a particular concept.

One of the challenges in developing a process to assess the impact of service-learning on students is the lack of proven effective methods available to evaluate this form of learning. Eyler and Giles (1994) claim that the lack of assessment instruments is due to the fact that the purpose of service-learning is not always delineated which results in ambiguous student variables, indicators, and outcomes. Universities define their service-learning programs with very different goals. Some are curricular based while others are strictly co-curricular. Some are concerned with social justice and citizenship development, while others are focused on using service-learning as a pedagogy directed to disciplinary course content. This diversity of programmatic goals makes the uniform assessment of service-learning outcomes very difficult if not impossible. As a result, educators have produced very few instruments that measure the impact that service has on students.

The authors of this monograph were faced with the challenge of assessing the impact service-learning was having on faculty, students, community partners, and the institutional culture. More specifically, we wanted to measure the impact of curricular based service-learning that is focused on enhancing classroom learning. Therefore, we developed a set of variables that described the impact on students and relevant indicators to measure this impact on students involved in service-learning projects connected to course content.

**Awareness of Community, Involvement in Community, Commitment to Service, and Sensitivity to Diversity** are all concepts that measure impact on students' psychological change. These psychological changes are indicated by students' increased knowledge of community issues and strengths, increased understanding of the role they play in addressing community concerns, and an increased sensitivity to working with communities that they have not previously been a part of. Although extremely important impact variables, these are all what Astin (1993) would call an *affective* student outcome.

- AWARENESS OF COMMUNITY seeks to determine if students had or developed a heightened awareness and understanding of community issues, needs, strengths, problems and resources.

- INVOLVEMENT WITH COMMUNITY describes the quality and quantity of interactions with the community, their positive or negative attitude about working with the community partner, a desire or importance of getting feedback from their community partner, and or a recognition about the benefits they gain and the community partner gain through their relationship.

- **COMMITMENT TO SERVICE** is measured by looking at students' attitudes toward their current service and their plans or barriers for future service.

- **SENSITIVITY TO DIVERSITY** is measured by students' expressed attitudes about working with communities with which they were not familiar, an increased comfort and confidence working within these communities, and a recognition that they gained knowledge of a new community.

Concepts such as **Career Development, Understanding of Course Content, and Communication** serve as measures of impact on students' cognitive development. As Eyler (2000) points out, it is extremely important to measure the impact on students' cognitive development because this is at the heart of most college and university missions. These concepts are indicated by students' ability to utilize the service-learning experience to influence their career decisions or give them the opportunity to develop skills that relate to those they will need in their intended career. Because the Portland State service-learning program is one that is primarily curricular-based, a particularly important concept to the Portland State research team was *Understanding of Course Content.* This concept is indicated by students' ability to apply what they are learning in the class to their community setting and their ability to understand how the service experience is relevant to the topic and learning goals of the class. One of the indicators for the *Communication* variable is students' increased skill development with the multiple communication demands of working within community settings. When students were able to demonstrate impact on any of these three concepts, clear cognitive change and growth could be documented.

- **CAREER DEVELOPMENT** is measured in terms of the development of professional skills and increased student awareness of the skills needed for a person working in the field in which they were doing their service project. This variable is also measured by students' increased knowledge about their career of interest (both positive and negative), as well as their understanding of the professional directions they might pursue.

- **UNDERSTANDING OF COURSE CONTENT** is measured by students' ability to make clear connections between the course goals and community based project.

- **COMMUNICATION** is measured by students' recognition that they may have gained new communication skills as well as the importance communication plays in the complex relationships presenting in these community based learning experiences.

**Self Awareness, Sense of Ownership, and Valuing of Multiple Teachers** are concepts that measure students' understanding of themselves as part of a learning community, and the skills and perspectives they themselves and their colleagues contribute to the community project and the class. The *Self-awareness* concept identifies when students recognize their own contributions, strengths and limitations regarding the community project in which they are engaged, as well as when they acknowledge that they have rethought and possibly modified previously held beliefs. *Sense of Ownership* measures students' recognition of themselves as contributors to a community of learners. Students may come to recognize that the community partner is a valuable source of knowledge, and that the partner looks to the students to contribute a high quality, valuable product at the conclusion of the course.

**Valuing of Multiple Teachers** addresses the fact that service-learning courses offer a different teaching modality than traditional classrooms, and students may recognize that student colleagues, community partners and their faculty play different and important roles in their learning in these experiences.

- SELF AWARENESS is measured by students' recognition and awareness of their own personal strengths and weaknesses as they relate to the completion of the course and their engagement in the community. This variable is also measured by the indication that a student changes his or her previously held beliefs due to his or her engagement in the community.

- SENSE OF OWNERSHIP is measured by students' expressed autonomy and independence from the faculty member. The student's ability to see his or her community partner as a source of knowledge and that student's increased investment in the class by taking responsibility to provide the community partner with high quality outcomes are all indicators of this variable.

- VALUING OF MULTIPLE TEACHERS is measured by students' descriptions of the changing roles among faculty, students, and community partners, as well as students' recognition that student peers and community partners may at times shift into teaching roles, while the faculty may occupy the role of learner.

## Strategies for Assessing Impact on Students

We articulated and designed measurement strategies most likely to gather useful and relevant data. Both qualitative and quantitative methods were necessary to learn about the different types of learning that was taking place. Creswell (1994) has advocated using an approach that incorporates multiple methods. Our approach to assessing service-learning has shown that combining methods proved to be useful as a strategy for enhancing validity of findings. We were able to triangulate the data by confirming findings from the student interview transcripts with observations in the classroom and the student survey. In addition, we were able to complement the data found in the surveys regarding students' perceptions about the impact of service-learning on future participation in the community with interviews from students. The interviews allowed students to describe various aspects of the data gathered in the survey in more depth. This was especially helpful when the information was personal, such as students becoming more aware of their own biases and prejudice. The interview quotes from the students made the statistical data more rich and descriptive of how these experiences affect students. In this process, researchers used the qualitative and quantitative approaches to expand the study to be inclusive of new concepts which students may have discovered through their service-learning experiences.

In addition to these stated purposes, the use of multiple data gathering methods allowed the Portland State research team to understand which of the methods would most likely provide useful and relevant data on the various concepts. With the less quantifiable psychological concepts, interviews and focus groups were methods by which students would explore perceptions of personal growth as it related to the service-learning course. Classroom observations, community observations, and surveys have the potential to capture the impact the service-learning experience had on students' cognitive skill development. As is the case with all of the data collected, in-person observations and individual and group interviews provide the researchers with the specific indicators of impact on students' cognitive growth that a survey may not capture. Given the chance to discuss and reflect on their skill development resulting from their involvement in the community, students provide a number of varied and specific examples.

## Surveys

ADVANTAGES OF SURVEYS: One of the greatest advantages to utilizing surveys as an assessment tool is the ease of analysis. Most institutions of higher education have an office of institutional research, or qualified faculty and staff trained to enter and analyze statistical data. This allows for the analysis of a wide range of courses, and also detailed analysis of data for specific research questions.

Surveys developed from this research are now used to collect data from more than 3,000 students per year at Portland State University. We are able to make substantive observations about the quality of service-learning courses, students' attitudes toward this pedagogy, students' perceptions of their learning, and their growth in each of the student concepts. We are also able to compare the impact that these courses have on students throughout the various levels of their education. For example, does participation in service-learning courses during the first year influence students in a different way than these types of courses in their senior year? Surveys also give us the ability to compare various forms of service-learning. Are students who engage in courses which contain direct contact with the community partner affected differently from those who do not come in direct contact with the community partner (perhaps by doing some form of indirect research project)? Finally, the surveys allow institutions to compare various populations, addressing such questions as: are non-traditional students affected in similar or different ways from traditional college age students? Do men and women respond differently to these courses? Surveys provide institutions the opportunity to analyze data from a large population and understand the impact of service-learning on the different types of students engaged in service.

LIMITATIONS OF SURVEYS: There are a few limitations to this method of data collection. First, the limitation of using the survey method alone is that it limits the amount of "student voice" in the assessment. Students are not given the opportunity to share their success, their personal struggles, or their own learning. Second, surveys frequently do not capture personal struggles and challenges faced in their community setting. Students often respond affirmatively to many of the questions, but when interviewed more fully describe an experience that often includes satisfactory and unsatisfactory encounters. Third, surveys do not allow students to describe the multiple factors that contribute to their evaluation of their learning experience. Fourth, surveys given too close to the end of a short-term service-learning experience may not fully capture the various impacts or changes in students' self-awareness. Therefore, we suggest using a blend of interviews and focus groups to add in depth understanding of the student experience.

## Interviews

**ADVANTAGES OF INTERVIEWS:** One advantage of the interview method is that it provides data regarding the context in which the student experience is taking place. For example students discuss how the community participation takes place in the context of their busy lives sometimes involving juggling multiple jobs and family responsibilities. In addition, interviews promote reflection — the hallmark of service-learning — and provide in-depth accounts of transformational events in the students' learning. Frequently these events take place as students encounter issues of race, class, gender, and difference in their communities. Interviews allow researchers to gain insights into the interactions that take place in these courses, the process of engaging with the community through the voices of students. Finally, the interview method provides solid and specific recommendations for improving the quality of service-learning courses. For example, the student interview protocol included in this monograph specifically introduces the notion of students' perceptions regarding their level of preparedness for the service experience they encountered. This information assisted administrators and faculty in planning ways to better prepare students for this type of work in the community. For example, as a result of data gathered through this method, administrators were able to identify the need for increased diversity training for students as they enter increasingly more ethnically and economically diverse communities.

**LIMITATIONS OF INTERVIEWS:** The primary limitation associated with the interview method is the labor-intensive task of analysis. Researchers can become bogged down in hundreds of pages of interview transcriptions and be faced with insufficient time, resources, and qualified staff to analyze the data. Institutions committed to learning about the student experience in service-learning courses need to allocate the proper level of resources to transcribe, analyze and write up the findings from the data. Designing interview protocols to focus on specific research variables and indicators provides a natural plan for analysis, and helps overcome this potential limitation.

## Focus Groups

**ADVANTAGES OF FOCUS GROUPS:** One major advantage of using focus groups is that they provide an opportunity for groups of students to reflect upon lessons learned in their experience and share this learning with others. Students gain new insights from hearing their peers share significant insights and struggles, and build connections between various ideas expressed by other students. Focus groups also allow researchers to capture student voices. As with student interview data, focus groups capture students' individualized experiences in the community. The researcher is able to ask probing questions that capture how the service-learning experience affected the student's learning. In addition, focus groups serve as a powerful way to reaffirm the learning that has taken place and to document the progress that has been accomplished in the course. They also serve as a means in which students can directly offer suggestions for improvement of the quality of the service-learning courses. Here, students are given the opportunity to demonstrate critical thinking skills as they offer constructive criticism and conceptualize programmatic improvements.

**LIMITATIONS OF FOCUS GROUPS:** There are a few disadvantages with the use of focus group data collection. 1) Focus groups require that students convene in one location, at a specified time, for a defined period. These logistical requirements can be difficult to organize since it is likely students will only be able to convene during the scheduled meeting time. Because of limited class time, giving up a class session to facilitate a focus group is not always possible. 2) Audio recording best captures focus group data. Having effective audio equipment that will uniformly capture the many voices of those participating in the focus group is an important, but often difficult technical challenge. 3) Like student interview data, analysis of focus group data can be a labor-intensive task that can easily burden researchers with many pages of transcriptions. 4) In classes where students do not have adequate time to reflect on their experience in the community, and do not have ample opportunity to discuss their community experience as it relates to the course content, focus groups provide an environment for students to discuss the logistical challenges of working in community-based settings. In a group setting like that of a focus group, once students begin discussing the logistical barriers to working in community settings turning the discussion to deeper analysis of learning can be very difficult.

## Concluding Thoughts

We have learned that collecting data through all of these methods allowed us to truly understand the dynamics of these complex courses. It gave us the means to triangulate data and to develop a solid sense of the impact on students (as well as on faculty, community partners, and the institution, as will be discussed in the subsequent sections). We are now able to utilize end-of-course surveys as a single proxy measure to understand impact when resources do not permit using other more labor-intensive methods (such as interviews and focus groups), and have developed the language to describe and effectively analyze the data from surveys.

# Table 5: Matrix for Student Assessment

| What do we want to know? (concepts) | How will we know it? (indicators) | How will we measure it? (methods examples) | Who/what will provide the data? (sources) |
|---|---|---|---|
| Awareness of community | Knowledge of community issues<br>Ability to identify community assets and needs<br>Understanding of community strengths, problems, resources | Interviews<br>Focus groups<br>Classroom observations | Students<br>Faculty<br>Community partners |
| Involvement with community | Quantity/quality of interactions<br>Attitude toward involvement<br>Interdependence among community partners and students<br>Feedback from community | Interviews<br>Focus groups<br>Classroom observations<br>Community observations | Students<br>Faculty<br>Community partners |
| Commitment to service | Attitude toward current service experience(s)<br>Plans for, and barriers to, future service<br>Reaction to demands/challenges of the service | Interviews<br>Focus groups<br>Surveys | Students<br>Faculty<br>Community partners |
| Career development | Career decisions/opportunities<br>Development of professional skills related to career<br>Opportunities for career preparation related to service experience | Surveys<br>Interviews<br>Focus groups | Students<br>Faculty<br>Community partners |
| Self-awareness | Awareness of personal strengths, limits, goals and fears<br>Changes in preconceived understandings/ability to articulate beliefs | Interviews<br>Surveys<br>Classroom observations | Students<br>Faculty<br>Community partners |
| Understanding of course content | Role of community experience in understanding and applying content<br>Perceived relevance of community experience to course content | Interviews<br>Surveys<br>Classroom observations | Students<br>Faculty<br>Community partners |
| Sensitivity to diversity | Attitudes about and understanding of diversity<br>Knowledge of new communities<br>Self-confidence and comfort in community settings | Interviews<br>Surveys<br>Community observations | Students<br>Faculty<br>Community partners |
| Sense of ownership | Autonomy and independence from faculty<br>Sense of role as learner and provider in partnership<br>Responsibility for community project | Focus groups<br>Classroom observations<br>Interviews | Students<br>Faculty<br>Community partners |
| Communication | Perceived skill development<br>Recognition of importance of communication<br>Demonstrated abilities (verbal and written) | Interviews<br>Classroom observations<br>Community observations | Students<br>Faculty<br>Community partners |
| Valuing of pedagogy of multiple teachers | Role of student peers in learning<br>Perception and role of community partners in learning<br>Role of faculty in learning | Focus groups<br>Classroom observations<br>Community observations | Students<br>Faculty<br>Community partners |

# Strategies and Methods: Students

## Student Survey

### Purpose

The student survey is intended to describe students' perspectives and attitudes on issues related to their experience in a service-learning course. The survey is based on a five point Likert scale where students report their level of agreement regarding their service-learning experience. The scale range includes "strongly disagree," "disagree," "neutral," "agree," and "strongly agree." Topics assessed through the survey include students' views or attitudes about service, the impact of the service on their choice of major/career and their understanding of the course material, their views on diversity issues, their perception of self-awareness, and the role other student colleagues and their community partner have in their learning. In addition, the survey provides demographic data, which profiles students' racial background, age, gender, class level, and employment.

The survey instrument is useful in describing students' perspectives and demographics that exist within one course and across courses in a university. With this standardized survey format, institutions are able to administer this survey to all service-learning courses. The data collected can be used by an individual faculty member to understand his or her student's perception about the impact that service-learning has on them. The data can also be collated to provide information that describes and measures the impact of service-learning institution-wide. Institutionally, surveys are one of the most efficient ways to collect information from a large number of students. Therefore, it is the one means that allows institutions to make claims about broad representation from the student body. This is useful for universities with diverse populations, especially those with a non-traditional student body. By utilizing this survey, faculty members and administrators will gain a profile of the student body they are serving.

Note that two survey instruments are included. One is a longer survey that was used initially in our work. Following the pilot testing, the survey was streamlined for administration and analysis through our institutional research office, and this scan-ready version is the second survey presented.

### Preparation

In preparation for using this instrument the following steps are recommended.

1. Faculty should determine if they are going to use this survey to assess change in students' perceptions and attitudes before and after the course, or if they are going to use the survey only to assess the general attitudes of the students after they have taken the course. The survey is meant to compliment other data-gathering strategies to develop a clearer picture of the students' perspectives and attitudes toward this form of learning.

2. Faculty should determine the most appropriate time to administer the survey. Pre-tests should be given in the first week of the academic term and post-tests in the last week.

3. Informed consent procedures should be initiated and completed prior to survey administration.

## Administration

1.  Faculty should stress the importance of the instrument so the students take the time to respond to the survey with honesty and integrity.

2.  Faculty and the researchers should also assure students that their response will not negatively or positively affect the faculty or community partner, or the students' grades.

3.  Student confidentiality should be assured and maintained throughout the collection of data.

4.  The survey should be handed out to students during a scheduled class time.

5.  Students should be given 15-20 minutes to complete the form.

6.  Forms should be collected before students leave the classroom.

7.  Results should immediately be shared with the participating faculty member.

## Analysis

Data analysis can be conducted through utilization of the Statistical Package for Social Sciences (SPSS) software. In the case of assessing and comparing pre- and post-service-learning experiences, the analysis could include frequencies and other descriptive statistics, Chi-squares, ANOVA, and factor analysis. Descriptive statistics can serve as a database, providing mean, mode, and standard deviation between items. Second, Chi-squares correlate demographic data between student groups. Third, Factor Analysis reduces items into categories that are closely related. Finally, Analyses of Variance or ANOVA's are useful to explore the existence of variation within and between groups on either single items or groups of items that may arise from the factor analysis. The descriptive data that provide a rich profile of the sample both in terms of demographics and responses to individual items are particularly useful.

The survey may be used in a pre/post format to measure change in the individual student. However, there are a few difficulties with the use of the pre/post surveys. First, it is difficult to measure significant change within a 10-week (quarter system) or 15-week (semester system) course. Few students will demonstrate dramatic changes in the concepts being assessed in one quarter or semester. Changes in attitudes about diversity, students' role as learners, and successful community development skills frequently take a full academic year to show significant movement. In addition to the short time frame, surveys have limited success in capturing individualized and personal student learning. Classroom observations, focus groups, and/or interviews with individual students may reveal significant change in student perceptions about their understanding of course content, awareness of their own personal development and strengths, and their choice of major/career. The pre/post survey does not reflect this change. As noted earlier, the survey data is most useful in collecting descriptive data from students.

**Community-Based Learning—Student Survey**

We would like to better understand the impact that community-based learning has on students. We particularly want to know how this experience has influenced your perspective on learning, your view of service, your choice of major/career, and your perspective of working in a diverse community.

1. **First, we would like to know some information about you.**

    1. What is your racial background?

        ❑ Caucasian/White        ❑ African American        ❑ Asian/Asian American
        ❑ Hispanic              ❑ Native American        ❑ Other

    2. What is your age group?

        ❑ Under 25        ❑ 25–34        ❑ 35–44        ❑ 45–54        ❑ Over 55

    3. What is your gender?        ❑ Male              ❑ Female

    4. What is your class level?   ❑ Freshmen          ❑ Sophomore          ❑ Junior
                                   ❑ Senior            ❑ Graduate Student   ❑ Other

    5. I have a job that requires  ❑ 1–10 hrs/wk       ❑ 11–20 hrs/wk       ❑ 21–30 hrs/wk
       me to work...               ❑ 31–40 hrs/wk      ❑ 41+ hrs/wk
                                   ❑ I do not have a job.

    6. Name of the community-based leaming course you enrolled in:_____

    7. The course number:_____

    8. Name of community partner/agency you worked with:_____

II. **Next, we would like to gain your perspective about this community-based learning course.**

   *Please indicate your level of agreement with each statement.*

|   | Strongly Disagree | Disagree | Neutral | Agree | Strongly Agree |
|---|---|---|---|---|---|
| 9. The community participation aspect of this course helped me to see how the subject matter I learned can be used in everyday life. | ❑ | ❑ | ❑ | ❑ | ❑ |
| 10. The community work I did through this course helped me to better understand the lectures and readings in this course. | ❑ | ❑ | ❑ | ❑ | ❑ |
| 11. I feel I would have learned more from this course if more time was spent in the classroom instead of doing community work. | ❑ | ❑ | ❑ | ❑ | ❑ |

| | Strongly Disagree | Disagree | Neutral | Agree | Strongly Agree |
|---|---|---|---|---|---|
| 12. The idea of combining work in the community with university coursework should be practiced in more classes at this university. | ❑ | ❑ | ❑ | ❑ | ❑ |
| 13. I was responsible for the quantity and the quality of knowledge that I obtained from this course. | ❑ | ❑ | ❑ | ❑ | ❑ |

III. The next set of questions relates to your attitude toward community involvement.

*Please indicate your level of agreement with each statement.*

| | Strongly Disagree | Disagree | Neutral | Agree | Strongly Agree |
|---|---|---|---|---|---|
| 14. I was already volunteering in my community before taking this course. | ❑ | ❑ | ❑ | ❑ | ❑ |
| 15. The community participation aspect of this course showed me how I can become more involved in my community. | ❑ | ❑ | ❑ | ❑ | ❑ |
| 16. I feel that the community work I did through this course benefited the community. | ❑ | ❑ | ❑ | ❑ | ❑ |
| 17. I probably won't volunteer or participate in the community after this course. | ❑ | ❑ | ❑ | ❑ | ❑ |
| 18. The community work involved in this course helped me to become more aware of the needs in my community. | ❑ | ❑ | ❑ | ❑ | ❑ |
| 19. I have a responsibility to serve my community. | ❑ | ❑ | ❑ | ❑ | ❑ |

IV. Next, we would like to know the influence of your service on your choice of major and profession.

*Please indicate your level of agreement with each statement.*

| | Strongly Disagree | Disagree | Neutral | Agree | Strongly Agree |
|---|---|---|---|---|---|
| 20. Doing work in the community helped me to define my personal strengths and weaknesses. | ❑ | ❑ | ❑ | ❑ | ❑ |
| 21. Performing work in the community helped me clarify which major I will pursue. | ❑ | ❑ | ❑ | ❑ | ❑ |

|  | Strongly Disagree | Disagree | Neutral | Agree | Strongly Agree |
|---|---|---|---|---|---|
| 22. The community work in this course assisted me in defining which profession I want to enter. | ❏ | ❏ | ❏ | ❏ | ❏ |
| 23. The work I accomplished in this course has made me more marketable in my chosen profession when I graduate. | ❏ | ❏ | ❏ | ❏ | ❏ |

## V. Finally, we would like some of your personal reflections on this experience.

*Please indicate your level of agreement with each statement.*

|  | Strongly Disagree | Disagree | Neutral | Agree | Strongly Agree |
|---|---|---|---|---|---|
| 24. Most people can make a difference in their community. | ❏ | ❏ | ❏ | ❏ | ❏ |
| 25. I developed a good relationship with the instructor of this course because of the community work we performed. | ❏ | ❏ | ❏ | ❏ | ❏ |
| 26. I was comfortable working with cultures other than my own. | ❏ | ❏ | ❏ | ❏ | ❏ |
| 27. The community work involved in this course made me aware of some of my own biases and prejudices. | ❏ | ❏ | ❏ | ❏ | ❏ |
| 28. The work I performed in this course helped me learn how to plan and complete a project. | ❏ | ❏ | ❏ | ❏ | ❏ |
| 29. Participating in the community helped me enhance my leadership skills. | ❏ | ❏ | ❏ | ❏ | ❏ |
| 30. The work I performed in the community enhanced my ability to communicate my ideas in a real world context. | ❏ | ❏ | ❏ | ❏ | ❏ |
| 31. I can make a difference in my community. | ❏ | ❏ | ❏ | ❏ | ❏ |

Finally, please add any other comments you have about courses where learning takes place in a community setting. (Please use the back of this piece of paper or attach an additional sheet of paper.)

*Thank you for your insights regarding community-based learning!*

## Community-Based Learning — Student Survey

We would like to better understand the impact that community-based learning has on students. We particularly want to know how this experience has influenced your perspective on learning, your view of service, your choice of career, and your perspectives on working with diverse communities. Please take 5-10 minutes to complete this survey, and return it before you leave class today.

### I. First we would like some information about you.

1. What is your ethnic background?

   ❑ Caucasian/White   ❑ African American   ❑ Asian/Asian American
   ❑ Hispanic          ❑ Native American    ❑ Other

2. What is your age group?

   ❑ Under 25      ❑ 25–34      ❑ 35–44      ❑ 45–54      ❑ Over 55

3. What is your gender?   ❑ Male       ❑ Female

4. What is your class level?   ❑ Freshmen     ❑ Sophomore          ❑ Junior
                               ❑ Senior       ❑ Graduate Student   ❑ Other

5. I have a job that requires   ❑ 1–10 hrs/wk       ❑ 11–20 hrs/wk      ❑ 21–30 hrs/wk
   me to work...                ❑ 31–40 hrs/wk      ❑ 41+ hrs/wk
                                ❑ I do not have a job.

6. Name of the agency/community organization with which you worked during this class: _____

### II. Next we would like to gain your perspective about this course. Please mark your level of agreement with each statement.

| | Strongly Agree | Agree | Neutral | Disagree | Strongly Disagree |
|---|---|---|---|---|---|
| 7. The community participation aspect of this course helped me to see how the subject matter I learned can be used in everyday life. | ❑ | ❑ | ❑ | ❑ | ❑ |
| 8. The community work I did helped me to better understand the lectures and readings in this course. | ❑ | ❑ | ❑ | ❑ | ❑ |
| 9. The idea of combining work in the community with university course work should be practiced in more courses at this university. | ❑ | ❑ | ❑ | ❑ | ❑ |

### III. The next set of questions relates to your attitude toward community involvement. Please indicate your level of agreement with each of the following statements.

| | Strongly Agree | Agree | Neutral | Disagree | Strongly Disagree |
|---|---|---|---|---|---|
| 10. I was already volunteering in the community before taking this course. | ❑ | ❑ | ❑ | ❑ | ❑ |
| 11. I feel that the community work I did through this course benefited the community. | ❑ | ❑ | ❑ | ❑ | ❑ |

|  | Strongly Agree | Agree | Neutral | Disagree | Strongly Disagree |
|---|---|---|---|---|---|
| 12. I was able to work directly with a community partner through this course. | ❏ | ❏ | ❏ | ❏ | ❏ |
| 13. I felt a personal responsibility to meet the needs of the community partner of this course. | ❏ | ❏ | ❏ | ❏ | ❏ |
| 14. I probably won't volunteer or participate in the community after this course. | ❏ | ❏ | ❏ | ❏ | ❏ |
| 15. My interactions with the community partner enhanced my learning in this course. | ❏ | ❏ | ❏ | ❏ | ❏ |

**IV. Next we would like to know about the influence of your service on your choice of major and profession.** *Please indicate your level of agreement with each of these statements.*

|  | Strongly Agree | Agree | Neutral | Disagree | Strongly Disagree |
|---|---|---|---|---|---|
| 16. Doing work in the community helped me to become aware of my personal strengths and weaknesses. | ❏ | ❏ | ❏ | ❏ | ❏ |
| 17. The community work in this course assisted me in clarifying my career plans. | ❏ | ❏ | ❏ | ❏ | ❏ |
| 18. The community work I performed in this class enhanced my relationship with the faculty member. | ❏ | ❏ | ❏ | ❏ | ❏ |
| 19. The community work involved in this course made me more aware of my own biases and prejudices. | ❏ | ❏ | ❏ | ❏ | ❏ |
| 20. The work I performed in the community enhanced my ability to communicate in a "real world" setting. | ❏ | ❏ | ❏ | ❏ | ❏ |
| 21. The community aspect of this course helped me to develop my problem-solving skills. | ❏ | ❏ | ❏ | ❏ | ❏ |

**V. Finally, we would like some of your personal reflections on this experience.**

|  | | | | | |
|---|---|---|---|---|---|
| 22. The syllabus provided for this course outlined the objectives of the community work in relation to the course objectives. | ❏ | ❏ | ❏ | ❏ | ❏ |
| 23. The other students in this class played an important role in my learning. | ❏ | ❏ | ❏ | ❏ | ❏ |
| 24. I had the opportunity in this course to periodically discuss my community work and its relationship to the course content. | ❏ | ❏ | ❏ | ❏ | ❏ |

*Thank you for your comments. Please return the completed form to [personalize information].*

## Student Interviews

### Purpose

Student interviews are intended to foster a one-on-one conversation with students to explore their experiences of working with the community in connection with an academic course. Interviews capture students' voices as they describe their experience of the service-learning course. This assessment method provides a deeper understanding of the nature of students' daily experiences in service-learning courses. Students state their own perception of the situations that they encountered and the meaning of these events in their lives.

The interview approach can be used to assess a wide range of effects of service-learning. Specifically, the interview protocol provided in this handbook is designed to gather data from students about the nature of their service-learning involvement, the student's role in these courses, their understanding about linkages between course content and the community, and the challenges of engaging in service-learning courses. Furthermore, it probes students' fears and concerns related to participation in the community, and assesses the self-awareness that emerges as a result of the experience.

### Preparation

Faculty should be asked to provide a class roster so the researcher may select a set of students to interview. If the students are doing different projects, faculty should be asked to help to identify students who are engaged in a range of varying projects. Informed consent procedures should be initiated and completing prior to beginning to arrange interviews. Schedule interviews with students who represent the diversity of community experience and background that make up the class. Begin contacting students and schedule a 1-hour interview with each in a location and at a time that is convenient to the student. In advance, describe the purpose of the interview so that the student may be prepared for the interview.

### Administration

The administration of interviews should be consistent across all interview subjects. The following guidelines will be useful for conducting interviews:

- Begin on time, introduce yourself and your role in the project, and explain the purposes of the interview

- Assure confidentiality and stress the importance of candor

- Assure the student that their faculty member or community partner will not be affected (negatively or positively) by their remarks

- Take notes or ask permission to tape record (assure the student that names will not appear on transcriptions)

- Follow the interview protocol carefully and keep probes neutral

If in the course of the interview you sense there are difficulties and challenges, encourage the student to discuss them by moving question 9 to the beginning of the interview.

## Analysis

Data analysis begins with transcription of interview tapes immediately after the interview. These transcriptions should be double-spaced for reading ease. An initial reading of the transcripts by several people will allow the analysis team to come up with a list of key words and themes that appear in the text, each of which may be coded with their own individual color or symbol. The key words and themes are compared and matched to the research variables. The research team should then read each of the transcribed interviews again to code each interview according to the agreed upon list of key words and themes. It is helpful to have multiple people independently reading, analyzing, and coding the interview data, so that these separate sources can be compared for consistency and accuracy. Once the data is coded, the individual interviews can be combined into research variable categories. This provides the researcher with a group of student quotes for each of the research variables. This data can be used to assess the level to which students have been affected according to each of the research variables.

Data analysis may also be completed by utilizing a qualitative data analysis package such as Ethnograph. Analysis may also be done by coding the interview data and categorizing transcribed text according to the set of research variables.

## Student Interview Protocol

*(Provide introduction to set context.)*

1. Describe the work you did in the community for this community-based learning course.

2. Describe your relationship with the community partner and the project.

3. What did you learn about the community through this experience? What did you learn in the community that connected to the content of this course? How was that connection made?

4. Did you have any fears or concerns about working in the community as part of this class? What were those concerns?

5. Do you think you will do anything differently as a result of your experience in this course? (Probe: volunteering, career choices, activism/advocacy, etc.?) Has this created any new opportunities for you?

6. What did you learn about yourself as a result of your experiences in this community-based course? (Probe: Did you become aware of biases or fears? What did this teach you about your interaction with people different than yourself?)

7. In your community-based learning course did you learn from anyone other than your faculty instructor? (Probe for: community partner, peers, other examples.)

8. Did you feel prepared to perform the work required of you? If not, what would have made you feel more prepared?

9. What did you find most challenging in your community service experience?

10. What did you find the most rewarding in your community service experience?

11. What would you change about this community-based course?

## Student Focus Groups

### Purpose

"Focus groups are fundamentally a way of listening to people and learning from them" (Morgan, 1998, p. 9). Focus groups can be used to stimulate an interactive discussion about service-learning experiences among students in a particular course. Data can be gathered regarding several student variables by discovering patterns of students' experiences. Students are queried through the focus group to learn how they define a successful service-learning experience and to gain insights about student interactions and relationships with community partners. The focus group should be structured with the intent of listening to suggestions for improvement in organizing and supporting students throughout their service-learning courses.

Students in focus groups will be able to provide feedback on various concepts by informing the researcher if certain variables were influenced through this experience. Secondly, data gathered from focus groups can improve planning for a service-learning program. Through focus groups, students can inform faculty and administrators about pitfalls in logistics, scheduling, and transportation necessary for effective planning in service programs. Thirdly, students can give feedback about the implementation of the course. Frequently students compare how this course was taught in relation to previous courses. They are able to discuss the different types of learning that took place. Finally, Morgan (1998) states that focus groups are effective for the purpose of final assessment, where data is used for quality improvement and students provide insights about "how and why" certain outcomes were achieved in the course. Students are able to utilize the focus group time to share with one another their final assessment of their service experience, and reflect on their varying community experiences and related learning outcomes with the researchers and their student colleagues.

### Preparation

Arrange with the course professor early in the quarter/semester for a one-hour session near the end of the term to conduct the focus group. The focus group should be scheduled during the usual class time and should take place after students have completed any final projects, papers, or tests to minimize distraction or frustration. Focus groups should be facilitated by independent researchers or experts. The faculty member should not be present.

Arrange for a quality tape recorder, preferably one with multiple omni-directional microphones. One facilitator will be needed for each 8-12 students. If the course is large, it may be necessary to divide the group, obtain a second room, get a second facilitator, and conduct two simultaneous focus groups. Each focus group should have a note-taker to accompany the facilitator. The note-taker should take responsibility for ensuring that the equipment is working continuously, turn the tape over when necessary, and take detailed notes about the conversation and non-verbal communication. In the event that the recording fails, the note-taker will be able to provide backup documentation of the focus group conversation.

## Administration

The introductory message on the following page should be read to the students prior to beginning the focus group questions. Some specific guidelines include:

- Remind students of the introductory guidelines as needed.

- Begin and end on time.

- Introduce facilitators and note-takers.

- Arrange the group in a circular form.

- The facilitator guides the discussion and is not a participant.

- Make sure all probing questions are neutral.

- Ensure that all students participate, no one dominates, and no one holds back.

- Remind students of the guidelines throughout the focus group discussion as necessary.

For more information on the administration of focus groups, see the citations for the work of David Morgan (1993, 1997, 1998) in the reference list.

## Analysis

Data analysis can be completed by utilizing a qualitative data analysis package such as Ethnograph or NUDIST (Miles & Huberman, 1994). Analysis may also be done by coding the focus group data by categorizing transcribed text according to the set of research variables.

Data analysis begins with transcription of interview tapes immediately after the interview. These transcriptions should be double-spaced for reading ease. An initial reading of the transcripts by several people will allow the analysis team to come up with a list of key words and themes that appear in the text, each of which may be coded with their own individual color or symbol. The key words and themes are compared and matched to the research variables. The research team should then read each of the transcribed focus group discussions again to code each according to the agreed upon list of key words and themes. It is helpful to have multiple people independently reading, analyzing, and coding the data, so that these separate sources can compare findings for consistency and accuracy. Once the data is coded, the individually coded focus group discussions can be combined into research variable categories. This provides the researcher with a group of student quotes for each of the key concepts. This data can be used to assess the extent to which students have been affected according to each of the concepts.

## Student Focus Group Protocol

### Introduction

Our goal for this focus group is to have an open and interactive discussion. Focus groups are a guided conversation in which everyone participates. We want to learn more about how you felt about your community-based learning experience and will ask you a few questions that will focus on aspects of the experience and its affect on you as a learner. As facilitator, I will be asking questions to guide the discussion, but will not be participating or offering my own comments or reactions.

The purpose of the focus group is to hear everyone's ideas and impressions. Generally, in a focus group, hearing what others say may stimulate your own thinking and reflection on your experience. You do not need to repeat what others have said, but rather offer your own unique view or expand, clarify, or elaborate on what others have said. If you hear comments or ideas with which you disagree, do not hesitate to describe your perspective or contradictory view. A focus group, however, is not meant to resolve those differences or to press for consensus. The idea is to hear everyone's thoughts, not to reach agreement. There are no right or wrong answers. The purpose is to capture a wide array of comments, opinions, ideas, and suggestions.

This discussion will be tape-recorded. Your faculty instructor will not hear the recording. Only the person transcribing the tape will hear it. The summary reports or transcripts will not identify speakers so what you say will be kept confidential. To ensure a quality transcription, it will be helpful if you speak one person at a time, and try to speak clearly and with more volume than usual so your comments are captured on tape.

### Questions

1. What were your own personal learning goals for this community-based learning experience? What were the learning goals of the class? (10 min.)

2. How would you assess your experience? Was it a success? Why? What factors contributed to the success? What obstacles did you encounter and how did you overcome them? (5 min.)

3. Describe your interactions with the community partner. What role did your community partner have in your learning? (10 min.)

4. What did you learn about the community or society in general from this experience? (10 min.)

5. Did this community experience leave you with new questions or concerns? (5 min.)

6. What connections can you describe between the community service work and the classroom discussions, required readings, assignments? Was there a good balance of course time and community activity? (10 min.)

7. What role did your instructor play in your community service work? (5 min.)

8. What recommendations do you have for future community-based learning courses? (5 min.)

9. Do you have any other comments you would like to share?

*Thank participants.*

# Faculty Impact

## Why Assess the Impact on Faculty?

Throughout the service-learning literature, there is repeated acknowledgement of the critical role and influence of faculty. As Bringle and Hatcher (1998) note, service-learning in its most common form is a course-driven feature of the curriculum, an area of the university that is controlled by faculty. The prominent features of quality service-learning or community-based learning depend for the most part on the faculty, including meaningful and adaptive placements, connections between subject matter and community issues, and experiences, critical reflection, and preparation for diversity and conflict (Eyler & Giles, 1999).

There is also growing indication of the resulting changes in the nature of faculty work influenced by the service-learning movement. As such learning becomes increasingly integrated into the broad spectrum of faculty roles and responsibilities and visibly institutionalized in higher education (Zlotkowski, 1999a), there are signs of its influence in the professional life of faculty. Thus, faculty are both influential with, and influenced by, service- or community-based learning.

As early as 1990, Stanton criticized the minimal attention given to the faculty role in service-learning literature (Stanton, 1990). Most of the current literature has focused on the preparation of faculty for service-learning (Bringle & Hatcher, 1995; Bringle & Hatcher, 1998; Stanton, 1994) and on institutional reward systems that support faculty work in service-learning (Driscoll & Lynton, 1999; Holland, 1997; Lynton, 1995). Yet we continue to know little about the relationship between faculty and service-learning.

Further study of faculty roles will help to better understand faculty perceptions, predict which faculty will embrace service-learning, and determine what resources are necessary to help prepare faculty for roles as community-based teachers. The faculty need to have a good sense of how service-learning relates to their discipline and specifically to course content, and also need an understanding of their role with respect to working with community partners. They also often need new skill development to create partnerships, design effective student assessment strategies for community-based learning, and integrate new methodologies such as reflection into their courses. Thus assessment of faculty can also help to understand the demands that this pedagogy places on faculty.

Holland (1999a) used multi-institutional data to outline the key factors that motivate faculty involvement in service, and to identify strategies for increasing motivation. With increased attention to the pedagogy of service or community-based learning, universities and colleges have begun to attend to motivating and supporting faculty as the "cornerstone for implementing service-learning" (Rice & Stacey, 1997).

The comprehensive case studies conducted at Portland State University (Driscoll, Holland, et al., 1996) addressed the gap in the service-learning literature by developing a range of strategies and methods for studying faculty. The case studies yielded significant core concepts, and aided subsequent revision of instrumentation for faculty, including a survey, interview protocol, classroom observation protocol, syllabus analysis guide, and a guide for analysis of curriculum vitae.

## Current State of Research on Faculty and Service-Learning

For reasons well known in higher education, major research and evaluation efforts have focused on student outcomes of service-learning (Astin & Sax, 1998; Berson & Younkin, 1998; Eyler & Giles, 1999). Evidence that service-learning makes a difference in students' educational experiences has significant implications for funding, resource allocation, program development, and institutional change. For some of the same reasons, there is intense interest in assessing the impact of service-learning on the community and the institution. In contrast, there has been a distinct lack of research focused on faculty and service-learning.

One notable exception to the gap in the service-learning literature is a study by Hammond (1994) of faculty motivation, satisfaction, and the intersection of the two. Commissioned by the Curriculum Development Committee of the Michigan Campus Compact, Hammond contacted 250 faculty in 23 Michigan institutions of higher learning to gather baseline data about the characteristics of faculty and the service-learning courses they were teaching. A survey was developed to document those characteristics and to query faculty about their service-learning work. Interestingly, the 163 survey respondents affirmed the importance of three conditions previously found to be related to general faculty satisfaction in academic culture (Astin & Gamson, 1993; Bess, 1982; Deci & Ryan, 1982; McKeachie, 1982): 1) sufficient freedom, autonomy, and control; 2) belief that their work has meaning and purpose; and 3) feedback that their efforts are successful. Hammond's study can inspire a significant but unrealized agenda focused on faculty roles and satisfaction in service-learning, pedagogical issues, and the faculty need for support.

The theme of faculty development has been studied with increasingly more attention as campuses became aware of the importance of the faculty role. Development efforts and research studies have focused on different dimensions of faculty in service-learning. Bringle and Hatcher (1995) addressed faculty cognitive needs with the assumption that a critical knowledge base is essential to the implementation of service-learning. In contrast, Ward (1996) proposed and supported the value of peer support. She stated, "The most effective person to encourage faculty to use service-learning as a pedagogical tool is a fellow member of the faculty who understands the cultural nuances of the campus (e.g., workload issues, relative weight of teaching to research)" (p. 33). Many campuses advocate the value of long-term efforts in faculty development to secure commitment and assure faculty that service-learning is not just another educational "fad"(Johnson, 1996). Finally, programs such as the Office of Academic Service-Learning Faculty Fellows Program at Eastern Michigan University developed and studied a small group dynamics model within a long-term faculty development approach to both prepare and educate faculty as well as to promote commitment to the pedagogy (Rice & Stacey, 1997). Their findings were positive about the faculty development approach while highlighting the need for ongoing development efforts and activities to sustain interest and involvement in service-learning and to recruit new faculty.

Faculty development was one of eight strategies for increasing faculty involvement in service and service-learning identified by Holland (1999a). Drawing upon interviews and focus groups with faculty members from 32 diverse institutions, Holland identified three primary types of motivational forces that affect faculty involvement: 1) personal values regarding social responsibilities; 2) relevance to their discipline; and 3) evidence of potential reward or other positive impact on the individual or institution. With these motivational forces in mind, Holland articulated key obstacles to increasing faculty commitment to service and reported on the most effective strategies for overcoming these barriers. Among the strategies for enhancing faculty motivation is the curriculum itself. Service-learning in the curriculum is often the first service-related activity that faculty members will try, and it has proven to be a good approach to building faculty confidence and interest in public service as academic work (Zlotkowski, 1999b).

Recent efforts to study and assess faculty roles in service-learning encourage and inspire the development of a future agenda that is holistic and attends to both the influence of faculty on service-learning and the impact of service-learning on faculty. The PSU case studies attended to the latter with the identification of core concepts of impact as well as the development of associated measurement methods. The core concepts also extended to current interest areas of professional development, motivation and attraction of faculty, satisfactions, and barriers and facilitators to begin to provide a wide lens with which to study the faculty role in service-learning.

## Assessment Matrix for Faculty Impact

The assessment matrix for faculty impact is presented in Table 6 and represents those core concepts that emerged from the PSU case studies as well as other research and descriptions of "best practice." Each of the concepts will be described with a rationale for its importance and a summary of what is known about the concept within the larger framework of service-learning and other community initiatives for faculty.

**Motivation and attraction of faculty to service-learning:** With the beginning work of Hammond (1994), Holland (1999a) and the PSU case studies (Driscoll, Holland, et al. 1996), we have begun to have an understanding of what brings faculty to service-learning and what sustains them. At the top of the list of motivators is the satisfaction faculty experience with service-learning as a pedagogy—the experience of observing students transformed by community work. That satisfaction affirms findings on faculty satisfaction with their work in general. With service-learning, there are new indicators of increased awareness about community context, and unique insights for both faculty and students that accompany the faculty involvement in community-based learning experiences. As with most faculty efforts, the importance of the reward system and institutional support are critical to motivating and attracting faculty.

Information about motivation and attraction of faculty to service-learning is critical to the institutionalization of service or community-based learning on campuses. The information will inform faculty recruitment and faculty development planning and programs.

**Professional development (support needed/sought):** Closely aligned with the attraction and motivation variable is a description of the professional development needs of faculty involved in service-learning. Again the institutionalization of service-learning depends on both attracting faculty and supporting them to sustain their involvement.

While there is growing literature about "what works" in faculty development related to service-learning, there has been minimal attention to studying professional development from the perspective of faculty needs — asking faculty and other constituencies about the kind of support needed by faculty. There is a strong indication that the satisfaction gained by faculty from their service-learning experiences as well as the level of impact they will have on students and community through facilitation of service-learning may depend greatly on the professional development support provided to them. This concept is of great significance to the success of most programs.

**Impact or influence on teaching:** As observed in the PSU case studies and noted by other service-learning practitioners (Howard, 1995; Driscoll, Strouse, & Longley, 1997; Gelmon, Holland, Shinnamon, & Morris, 1998), service or community-based learning has the potential to change faculty pedagogy significantly. Both faculty and students have access to new information through their involvement with the community as well as new resources for learning. The unexpected and unanticipated events, ideas, questions, and interests of community work have the potential to revise curriculum, modify teaching methods, and even transform the roles of faculty and students.

Information about the impact of service-learning on the teaching of faculty is of great interest to campuses with a commitment to enhanced student learning. Many of the changes in faculty teaching observed in service-learning contexts are correlated with increases in student engagement and achievement. For many campuses, institutional missions are directed to student outcomes of civic engagement and responsible citizenship, so that faculty pedagogy is again critical to achieving those missions.

**Impact or influence on scholarship:** For many faculty, especially junior or untenured faculty, this area of impact is most significant. Participating in service- or community-based learning takes a toll on faculty time, realistically adding responsibilities to those typically associated with teaching. These time demands can add stress to a situation in which many faculty already feel vulnerable; thus, there is the potential for negative impact on faculty scholarship. On the other hand, participation in service- or community-based learning can open new venues for faculty scholarship with the potential for positive impact on faculty scholarship. New areas of research, new publication foci, and scholarly collaborations with colleagues and community partners all offer potential for faculty rewards.

Those faculty who do succeed in building scholarship around community-based learning provide models to colleagues and more importantly promote institutional change around faculty roles and rewards. This concept has the potential to transform campus culture as well as national initiatives. Currently, many professional disciplinary associations support new forms of scholarship and provide credible venues for faculty work (Zlotkowski, 2000). As the service-learning movement grows and becomes nationally institutionalized, the impact on faculty scholarship will gain in importance and contribute much to the movement.

**Other personal or professional impact:** This category of impact possibilities emerged as we identified unanticipated kinds of impact on faculty. Within this category are the possibilities for enhanced faculty volunteerism because of their experience with service-learning, as well as new roles for faculty within community organizations. For many institutions of higher education, these possibilities will make strong contributions to their missions of civic engagement.

Within the pedagogical experience, there is potential for new or different mentoring roles with students. Connecting academic content with community-based projects often changes the roles of faculty and students, reveals different needs of students, and/or enhances the relationships between faculty and students. Thus, faculty may begin to interact with students in non-traditional ways or through enhanced mentoring.

Because service-learning is still novel and considered an innovation on many campuses, faculty involvement often leads to leadership roles for those participating faculty. They may become the unofficial champions or advocates for the campus with the potential to influence their peers. Ultimately, most faculty develop a deep commitment to service-learning after several experiences with this pedagogy.

**Barriers and facilitators:** Much like our findings about motivation and attraction, the information about barriers and facilitators to faculty participation in service-learning is critical to campus programs of recruitment, faculty development, and support. The increased time demands and responsibilities that come with teaching a service-learning course mean there is a need to identify barriers and provide needed support to ease or remove those obstacles to faculty success. Similarly, the need to identify facilitators and ways to support or ease the workload of faculty in service-learning courses are essential to both individual success and campus success. As faculty gain experience with service-learning courses, their awareness of barriers and facilitators can be captured through assessment activities and used to guide institutional decisions and actions.

This concept will no doubt be expanded as we develop extended experience with service-learning and study its use in different settings of higher education. It will hold individual possibilities as well as institutional possibilities in terms of specific findings and will further inform infrastructure and resource decisions in the future.

**Satisfaction with the experience:** This too is a concept that offers present and future potential for study. Our early findings reveal much satisfaction with the pedagogical aspects of service-learning—the joys of student learning experiences and new insights, the extended outcomes for student learning, and the commitment of students to community work following a service-learning course. All of these provide enormous satisfaction for faculty. We have observed the collegiality built into campus programs for faculty participants in service-learning and the satisfaction of being involved with such programs.

The insights of individual faculty are critically important to the satisfaction concept. At the same time, developing profiles of faculty satisfaction informs faculty recruitment, support for faculty, faculty development, and reward systems to ultimately enhance institutional engagement with the community.

In sum, all of the faculty concepts have enormous potential to shape and support the institutionalization of service-learning on individual campuses and nationally. The information provided by studying each of the variables will enhance the work of faculty in service-learning and ultimately make service-learning an integral component of every student's higher education experience.

## Strategies for Assessing Impact of Service-learning on Faculty

When developing and implementing strategies to study faculty in service-learning contexts or to assess the impact of service-learning on faculty, considerations of time, sensitivity to faculty workload, convenience of scheduling, and confidentiality issues must be maintained. When designing strategies to assess impact on faculty, researchers experience difficulty in developing approaches that are non-intrusive and that view impact holistically. We have used multiple sources of evidence from a range of strategies in order to capture a "big picture" of impact and to reveal unexpected concepts. Once data is collected, the varied sources of evidence can be triangulated, with each set of data explained, clarified, or extended by the information provided by another source of data. For example, insights gained from faculty interviews helped explain what was observed in the faculty member's classroom or reviewed in the curriculum vitae. Similarly, faculty insights about a course experience can be augmented by additional review of student and community observations of the same experience.

The accuracy of information gained from strategies to assess the impact of service-learning on faculty depends on the questions posed, the availability of faculty to participate in the assessment activities, and on the resources available for assessment. We have found that significant change in faculty-expressed attitudes or observations of behavior are not usually evident during a typical academic quarter or semester; thus, there is a need for extended studies and long-term assessment. Similarly, some assessment concepts, such as scholarship, will not be evident over the short-term, and will evolve over a number of years.

These strategies to assess impact on faculty are best used in combination. They provide substantive data when used for multiple forms of evidence, and offer a blend of opportunities to solicit the faculty voice (faculty interview and survey), to observe the faculty work (classroom observation), and to review faculty documentation (syllabus analysis, curriculum vitae analysis). They provide both quantitative and qualitative data that yield a profile of individual faculty or a composite of a group of faculty.

## Faculty Survey

**BENEFITS OF THE FACULTY SURVEY:** The faculty survey is designed for use as a post-test after faculty have completed their teaching of a service-learning course. As a post-test, the survey provides a profile of faculty who are teaching service-learning courses. The survey can also be modified as a pre-test instrument to use in a pre-post study for assessing change in faculty attitudes and perceptions.

**ISSUES WITH USE OF THE FACULTY SURVEY:** Much of the survey is designed with "forced choice" items and may not always provide the most accurate data. It does not provide much opportunity for explanation of faculty responses so there is a chance for misinterpretation. When used as a pre-post test in a traditional academic quarter or semester, the time period may be too brief for any significant change to be indicated. It may be best used before and after a faculty member has taught a service-learning course two or three times.

## Faculty Interview

**BENEFITS OF THE FACULTY INTERVIEW:** The faculty interview has multiple uses for both individual faculty members and for institutions and programs. It can be used as a reflective process to assist faculty in reviewing and assessing their experience and course. In its narrative form, it can be used to support individual scholarship of engagement. The faculty interview also provides an opportunity for faculty to provide input and insights to the campus program. Data can be used for planning faculty development, for making decisions about resource allocation, and for assessing campus-wide impact of service-learning. The faculty interview is best used as a complement to the faculty survey, as well as with observational data and the analysis of faculty vitae.

**ISSUES WITH FACULTY INTERVIEW:** Care must be taken to ensure confidentiality and the interviewee's capacity to be candid by assuring that the interviewer is someone who will not be a threat or cause discomfort to the interviewee. Care must also be taken to assure that all interviews are conducted with consistency in the procedures and the questions, and use only neutral probes. The interviewer must not comment on the responses of the interviewee.

## Classroom Observation

**BENEFITS OF CLASSROOM OBSERVATION:** Initially the data gained from classroom observations captures the status of service or community integration in academic courses. As such it can guide faculty development planning and campus programs. It can also yield a campus profile of teaching and learning when used with a significant number of faculty.

For individual faculty, data from classroom observations provides information useful for self-assessment of teaching and appropriate for submission as scholarship of engagement or scholarship of teaching or both. Observations allow the researcher to report to the faculty member about the demonstrable learning of students.

**ISSUES WITH USE OF CLASSROOM OBSERVATION:** Classroom observation data collection is both time-consuming and costly, but does yield data that describes multiple aspects of service-learning within a course context. Such observations capture the dynamics of the teaching and learning processes with complex and comprehensive data. Observer training is critical and must be conducted with attention to reliability. The analysis process is also time-consuming and requires skills to surface both the expected patterns as well as the unexpected themes. It is often suggested that two different individuals analyze the same classroom observation data to better probe all of the patterns.

By listening to classroom discussions the researcher is able to document student quotes regarding their reaction to a community issue being studied, their personal response to engaging in the community, and observe the "teachable moments" that take place as faculty and students come together to make meaning out of the experience. Classroom observations allow the researcher to assess the level to which the service experience is being integrated into the discussion of the class content. This first hand observation also allows the researcher to track the impact that the service experience has on the way the faculty teaches the class. These elements are only observable and trackable when the researcher has first hand access to students and faculty interacting.

A few of the disadvantages of classroom observations are: 1) it can be difficult to gain access to classes because faculty may not feel comfortable allowing a researcher to observe their teaching; 2) the researcher who observes the class on a periodic basis can become intrusive to the class dynamics and culture, causing the faculty or students to behave differently; and 3) for classroom observation to be an effective source of data, the researcher must be available to attend class frequently to stay abreast of the dynamics of the class and those critical events occurring in the community. These frequent observations cause this form of data collection to be time-consuming and labor intensive.

## Teaching/Learning Continua

BENEFITS OF THE TEACHING/LEARNING CONTINUA: The uses of the teaching-learning continua are quite similar to those of classroom observations in general. They have uses at all levels: individual faculty, program, and institutional. The continua capture unique and specific qualities of teaching and learning, rather than general observational data. The continua should be used in conjunction with the observation protocol.

In addition to being used by observers in describing individual class sessions, ongoing classes, and change or lack of change in teaching and learning, the continua can be used as a self-assessment or reflection tool by individual faculty. They can also be used by students to reflect on or provide feedback on individual class sessions or as an ongoing form of feedback. If they are used by students, it is imperative that students understand the concepts and terms used in the continua, which adds another kind of content to a course. The kinds of understandings implied in the continua could enhance students' meta-cognitive learning.

ISSUES WITH USING THE TEACHING/LEARNING CONTINUA: The accuracy of use of the teaching/learning continua increases with consistent understanding of the continua's concepts. Without thorough discussion and development of definitions and understandings of the concepts, the data from observations may be misleading or inaccurate. The discussions and development processes are, however, very useful and valuable for those participating in a service-learning program.

When the continua are used as a self-assessment or reflection tool by faculty or students, there is a tendency for users to place themselves on the lines where they think they "should" be. The concepts are not value-free, so there is the potential for values to influence the respondents' choices. However, another positive implication of this issue is that respondents, especially faculty, may be influenced behaviorally by their own responses, and modify their own teaching.

## Syllabus Analysis

BENEFITS OF SYLLABUS ANALYSIS: The syllabus analysis guide is useful for the initial development of a syllabus, or the review and modification of a syllabus. Used with other assessment processes, syllabus analysis can provide a profile of an individual course or of a faculty member's approach to service-learning. The syllabus analysis is also evidence of the scholarship of engagement or the scholarship of teaching or both, and is thus useful for the individual faculty member's professional portfolio. Use of the syllabus analysis guide is a valuable faculty development process when used by the individual faculty member or a group of faculty.

ISSUES IN USING THE SYLLABUS ANALYSIS: The previously mentioned sensitivities and time needed for both design and analysis of faculty syllabi will be important to attend to during the entire process. In analyzing a syllabus, care must be taken not to impose on the faculty member's disciplinary expertise, but rather to focus on how the syllabus documents the nature and effort of a community-based learning experience. Areas to be examined include presence of specific objectives for the community experience, description of the use of reflection, ways in which course and community content is integrated, and methods for assessment of student learning in the context of community effort.

## Faculty Journals

BENEFITS OF FACULTY JOURNALS: The faculty journal is best used in conjunction with other data gathering strategies focused on faculty teaching and learning. It will contribute insights and perspectives for individual faculty profiles as well as information and direction for program planning. Journals help faculty to engage in their own reflection as it relates to service-learning and can give faculty the necessary experience to help students with their own journal writing.

Individual faculty may use their journal narratives in the development of the typical narratives used in promotion and tenure portfolios. Journals will reveal faculty struggles in making connections between course content and community activities. They may also help faculty to identify the difficulties they might experience with classroom exchanges related to project content and challenges.

ISSUES WITH USING FACULTY JOURNALS: It is almost impossible to guarantee anonymity when analyzing faculty journals because the writing often reveals circumstances and details that identify individuals. Individual faculty should be alerted to this issue and assured that all possible steps to protect their anonymity will be taken in the reporting of findings. Faculty should be encouraged to re-read their journal entries prior to submission for analysis, and to disguise information that is too personal, revealing, or confidential to share.

Faculty journals are also time-consuming and it is often difficult for faculty to consistently write in them. Analysis of the journal data is equally time-consuming. Both processes have significant merit and ultimately warrant the time investment.

### Curriculum vitae analysis

BENEFITS OF CURRICULUM VITAE ANALYSIS: The curriculum vitae analysis and guide may be used by individual faculty members in preparation of their materials for promotion and tenure review and documentation of their scholarly activities related to community service. The guide supports reflection by individual faculty on their professional and scholarly activities during the preparation and documentation process.

The curriculum vitae analysis and guide may also be used to study faculty who are engaged in service and community-based learning. It can provide an individual profile or a composite of a group of faculty's scholarly activities related to community service. The information may be used to plan faculty development on an individual or group level, as well as to support faculty scholarship. Further analysis will provide evaluation information on the roles of faculty in community.

## Concluding Comments

The time and resources required for conscientious assessment of impact on faculty may look daunting but the "future growth and sustainability of service-learning depends to a large extent on the faculty, and the success with which universities are able to support and reward their efforts" (Driscoll, 2000, p. 39). Careful and systematic assessment of the impact on faculty and their impact on service-learning offers an opportunity for "scholarly study of faculty work with the end result of more informed decision making, programmatic changes, and directions for resources and efforts" (p. 40). For faculty in general, the assessment will enhance higher education's understanding of their roles, their work, and their needs for support. For individual faculty, the assessment process as well as the data from such assessments can foster more reflective practice.

# Table 6: Matrix for Faculty Assessment

| What do we want to know? (concepts or variables) | How will we know it? (indicators) | How will we measure it? (methods) | Who/what will provide the data? (sources) |
|---|---|---|---|
| Motivation and attraction of faculty to service-learning | Level and nature of community participation<br>Activity related to level of learner in courses/discipline<br>Linkage to other scholarly activities<br>Identification of motivating factors (value, rewards, etc.)<br>Awareness of socioeconomic, environmental, cultural factors | Interviews<br>Focus groups<br>Critical incident review<br>Curriculum vitae analysis | Faculty<br>Students<br>Community partner<br>Department chair<br>Faculty peers |
| Professional development (support needed/sought) | Attendance at related conferences/seminars<br>Participation in campus-based activities<br>Leadership/mentoring role with others in promoting SL<br>Role in advocating service-learning in academic societies | Interview<br>Focus groups<br>Curriculum vitae analysis | Faculty<br>Community partner<br>Students |
| Impact or influence on teaching | Knowledge of community assets and needs<br>Nature of class format, organization, activities<br>Evolution of teaching and learning methods<br>Articulation of philosophy of teaching<br>Nature of faculty/student/community partner interactions | Interview<br>Focus groups<br>Critical incident review<br>Curriculum vitae analysis | Faculty<br>Community partner<br>Students<br>Institutional resources |
| Impact or influence on scholarship | Changes in research emphases<br>Changes in publication/presentation content and venues<br>Changes in focus of research proposals, grants, and projects<br>Scholarly collaborations around community-based learning | Interview<br>Focus groups<br>Critical incident review<br>Curriculum vitae analysis | Faculty<br>Community partner<br>Institutional resources |
| Other personal or professional impact | Creation of partnerships with community organizations<br>New roles with community organizations<br>Campus-based leadership role around CBL<br>Mentoring of students<br>Commitment to community-based teaching and learning<br>Role in department/program advocating service-learning | Interview<br>Focus groups<br>Critical incident review | Faculty<br>Community partner<br>Students<br>Department chair |
| Identification of barriers and facilitators | Strategies to capitalize on facilitators<br>Methods and activities to overcome barriers<br>Illustrations of creative problem-solving<br>Ability to build upon barriers and create facilitators | Interview<br>Focus group<br>Critical incident review | Faculty<br>Community partner<br>Students |
| Satisfaction with experience | Strengths and lessons learned<br>Opportunities for improvement for future | Interview<br>Focus groups | Faculty<br>Students |

# Strategies and Methods: Faculty

## Faculty Interviews

### Purpose

Faculty interviews are intended to foster one-on-one conversation with faculty members to explore their perspectives on the experience of connecting the academic content of a course to community service. This approach could be used to assess a wide variety of possible outcomes for faculty engaged in service- or community-based learning. This interview protocol is designed to probe community awareness, teaching and learning philosophy and practice, the logistics of service-learning, and influences of the community service experience on faculty work in general.

### Preparation

The following steps are recommended in advance of the actual administration:

1. Identify and schedule a location with minimal distraction and maximum comfort.

2. Schedule the interview at a time and location convenient to the faculty member.

3. Advise the faculty member of the purpose of the interview so that they may reflect on impact and related issues in advance of the interview session. Gain consent to tape record the interview.

4. Review the interview protocol to ensure smooth administration of the questions.

### Administration

Once preparation is complete, the following guidelines are recommended for the interview:

1. Begin on time.

2. Introduce yourself and your role in the assessment process.

3. Explain the purposes of the interview and respond to the faculty member's questions.

4. Assure confidentiality.

5. Stress importance of candor.

6. Tape record the interview (with permission), and also take back-up notes.

7. Follow the interview protocol carefully and keep probes neutral.

### Analysis

Before analysis of the data, a careful transcription of tape recordings is necessary as well as a review of notes taken during the interview. The transcribed notes should be read at least two times before any analysis occurs. After several readings, the reader identifies key words and themes. These key words and themes are then coded on the transcripts. The key words and themes are further organized into patterns and related to the research variables. There may be key words and themes that indicate new variables or unexpected patterns.

## Faculty Interview Protocol

*(Provide introduction to set context.)*

1.  Describe the conditions and needs of the community where the service-learning experience took place.

2.  Describe any new information you have learned about your community in the process of offering your community-based learning course.

3.  After teaching your community-based learning course, how would you describe your own learning experience?

4.  As you taught your community-based learning course, what were your concerns? How did you address them?

5.  Describe the preparation and coordination that this community-based learning course required.

6.  Was this a successful teaching and learning experience? How did you know?

7.  Were the student learning outcomes different in this course from those in courses without a community experience?

8.  Do you think that your teaching changed as a result of having a community dimension in your course? Why or why not?

9.  Based on this experience, when you teach another community-based learning course, how will you approach it?

10. Has your community-based learning experience influenced your other scholarly activities? Will it do so in the future?

11. Is there any other information you would like to share?

Thank the interviewee for their time and input.

# Syllabus Analysis

## Purpose

The purpose of the syllabus analysis and the accompanying guide is to provide a framework for the development and assessment of syllabi for service- or community-based learning courses. Within the analysis, aspects of a course can be highlighted: integration of community service, outcomes related to community service, assessment of community service outcomes, and major forms of pedagogy. The syllabus analysis facilitates assessment of one aspect of a course, providing a picture of the planning and thinking of a faculty member prior to teaching the course.

## Preparation

The most critical aspect of preparation for use of the syllabus analysis guide is adequate time in advance for the faculty member to study the guide and prepare or revise a syllabus for review. It is useful to bring faculty together to discuss the guide, explore the rationale for the components of the guide, and raise questions of the meaning or value of the components. It may be useful to provide expert consultation during this time to assist and illustrate examples of syllabus design and adaptation for service-learning.

It will be important during the preparation and administration to maintain sensitivity to individual faculty philosophies and approaches to course planning. Faculty have individual philosophies about the level of specificity of a syllabus, with some who prefer it loose and open to ongoing change and those who prefer a tightly constructed and organized document. If, however, the syllabus is to be used as a method of documentation for assessment, then it is necessary that there be some standardization of content to demonstrate the expression of service-learning components.

## Administration

Once faculty have been briefed on the format of the guide and engaged in discussions, they should be given adequate time to develop or review a syllabus before submission. Faculty can be given the option to simply submit the syllabus in writing or electronically or to present the syllabus orally with the opportunity to discuss, describe, or respond to questions about the components.

## Syllabus Analysis Guide

This guide is intended to identify the components of course design in general and the components of "best practices" in service- or community-based learning in particular. Using the guide for analysis purposes, the presence or absence of those components is highlighted, along with descriptions of how they are integrated in the course.

The main components expected in a syllabus for a service-learning course are:

1. Description of the service-learning experience.

2. Goals and objectives of the service-learning, and anticipated outcomes of the experiences for both students and for the community partner organization.

3. Opportunities for structured and unstructured reflections by students on the connections between academic content and community service.

4. Integration of academic content and community service in both teaching and assessment.

To determine the presence of these main components, the analysis looks for the following:

1. Course description which includes description of community-based learning experience and approach for the course.

2. Learning objectives or outcomes for students that are directly related to the community service component.

3. General service outcomes for community partners.

4. Nature of projects/assignments related to the community service experience.

5. Readings/discussions/presentations/speakers related to the community service experience.

6. Direct and deliberate connections between the academic content and the community service experience.

7. Opportunities for reflection, both structured and unstructured, in the form of assignments, journal writing, discussions, and other mechanisms explicitly described in the syllabus.

8. Assessment of community service experience as an explicit component of determining course evaluation and grade.

9. Evidence of the community service experience as a teaching/learning approach that is integrated with other pedagogy.

*Note:* There is no explicit weighting of these components. However, the ideal syllabus would include all of the components.

## Faculty Journal

### Purpose

The purpose of the journal is to encourage faculty through a structured opportunity to reflect on their experiences with service- or community-based teaching and learning. Many faculty already keep journals so this may not be a new experience for them. In this context, the journal may provide additional detail for developing profiles of faculty who teach service-learning courses. If faculty are willing to share their journals, the writing will provide data on issues, concerns, questions, successes, insights, and perspectives of the teaching and learning experience. Such content will be useful to the individual faculty member to review for self-assessment and summative reflection.

### Preparation and Administration

It is useful to bring faculty together, hold discussions of experiences with journal writing, and review the specific protocol for this activity. Faculty who are new to journal writing may have concerns and questions, and may need some additional coaching on the journal writing process and its merits.

In most cases faculty are asked to write in their journals every week of their course. Specific instructions are provided in the protocol to guide the content of the journal, as well as to focus specific entries. It is particularly important to emphasize to faculty that the intent of the journal is not to keep a diary of events and happenings, but to provide structured reflection on the events, on student learning, on personal learning, and on the ultimate achievement of course goals. It is useful to collect journals halfway through the course or period of study in order to provide feedback to faculty and if necessary to assist them in reflective writing rather than reporting. Copies of the final journals are then collected at the end of the course.

### Analysis

The analysis of faculty journals requires the same rereading process described for analyzing the data from faculty interviews and classroom observations. Again, the reader is searching for key terms and themes in the journals, to be later categorized into patterns. The journal data may be used to explain data gained from classroom observations or to elaborate on data from the faculty interviews. There is the potential for some quantitative data in the form of "over 50 percent of the entries" or "the theme appeared in six of the ten entries" to accompany the descriptive data of themes or patterns.

There is some value in simultaneous analysis of faculty journals with faculty interviews and classroom observations for the purpose of finding common themes and patterns, or connecting themes between the different sources of data.

## Faculty Journal Protocol

The purpose of keeping a journal is to offer a structured opportunity to reflect on experiences with service- or community-based teaching and learning. For purposes of discussing the process and value of journals, we will meet at the beginning of the semester [or quarter].

We ask you to hand in your journal twice during the semester [or quarter]: halfway through your course, and at the end of the course. We will provide feedback on the first half to guide your future journal writing. This feedback will not be about specific content, but rather about the connections you are making between your service-learning course and the key concepts we are interested in understanding.

Each week of the course, we ask you to write one to four pages in a journal, and in your writing to reflect on the community-based learning component of your course and its influence on your course in general. We encourage you to notice any changes in your role or orientation toward teaching and learning. Your reflection should address the following broad themes:

- VALUES: your own and those of your students about the community and the service-learning process

- YOUR ROLE AS A TEACHER AND LEARNER: any changes in those roles as a result of the service component and the community emphasis of the course

- SERVICE: your perspective on your personal commitment to service, your definition and awareness of your community, the service that you and your students are providing to the community, and the impact of the service on your course and teaching

- INFLUENCE ON SCHOLARSHIP: the impact (if any) that the community experience is having on the focus of your scholarly activities such as writing, presentations, research, and professional involvements

- MOTIVATION: personal motivation or incentive to create community-based or service experiences in this course

You may or may not address each theme in each entry. We urge you to explore other themes that emerge from your experiences.

### First Entry

Begin your first journal entry with an overview of the course you have planned, emphasizing the community-based service experience component. Set out a series of goals or desired outcomes you wish to achieve with respect to incorporating community-based teaching and learning into your course. After addressing the broad themes, develop a brief summary of the entry.

### Subsequent Entries

Each entry should be dated. Each week review your summary from the end of the previous week's entry and begin your new entry by commenting on the progress or changes from the previous entry and acknowledging any problems encountered. At the end of each weekly entry, reserve some space to discuss accomplishments of the week, anticipated challenges in the next week, and specific goals and actions to help you meet those goals.

## Last Journal Entry

At the end of the course, reread the entire journal and write a summary entry addressing the themes previously described. Comment on the extent to which your goals and desired outcomes were achieved and the personal and professional impact of the experience. Finally reflect on what you will do differently in the future as a result of this experience.

## Final Journal Reflection

This reflection will be structured around the format of the application for the Thomas Ehrlich Faculty Award for Service-Learning (presented annually by Campus Compact) and will summarize your reflections on your experience. You are asked to write a two-page reflective synthesis which describes how you integrate service- or community-based learning into your teaching, curricula, and scholarship and how you are or might be able to integrate academic and personal service.

Finally, please review all of your writing prior to submission, and "blind" or disguise any names or events that you feel are too sensitive or of a confidential nature. We will not reveal your name in any of our analysis, but if you are concerned that any of your writing is too private to disclose, then you should make changes (or delete that material) so that there are no potential opportunities for violation of privacy.

## Curriculum Vitae Analysis

### Purpose

Faculty members engaged in service- or community-based learning may illustrate this activity and related scholarship in their curriculum vitae. The guide that accompanies this data gathering strategy provides a list of possible scholarly activities or contributions that faculty may include in their vitae. The list suggests possibilities for faculty consideration, but is not inclusive of the variety of scholarship possible when a faculty member is engaged in community activities. The curriculum vitae analysis contributes additional information to the faculty profile to which other data gathering strategies previously described are directed. It is designed to indicate and describe the influence of community engagement in the professional activities of faculty members.

### Preparation and Administration

Before the guide is used by individual faculty members, a review of the existing university guidelines is critical. Even with clear institutional guidelines for preparation of faculty curriculum vitae, the guide can suggest areas where a faculty member can document and highlight their community-based teaching and learning. The guide is best shared with both university and departmental administration as well as individual faculty. It is important to determine whether there are any areas of the guide that require modification to conform to university standards.

After presentation of the guide to faculty, group or private discussions may be useful to suggest how the individual faculty member's activities are best represented in the vitae. Peer suggestions and review will be very valuable in the process. Adequate time must be given for faculty to receive feedback and to revise their vitae before the final analysis (or submission of a personal dossier for review).

### Analysis

Once the vitae to be analyzed have been collected, the following procedures are recommended:

- A review sheet that includes the items in the guide is prepared.

- For each vitae analysis, the presence and absence of the items are noted with comments.

- Feedback is provided to the individual faculty members so that revisions can be made.

## Curriculum Vitae Analysis Guide

The impact of faculty engagement in community-based teaching and learning can be documented in multiple forms and in different categories of scholarship. The following suggested items of evidence are possible forms of scholarship related to service- or community-based learning:

### Teaching

1. Evidence of integration of community service into courses.

2. Achievements and recognition (by university or community) related to community-based teaching and learning.

3. Curriculum development projects (on an individual course level or departmental program level) related to community-based teaching and learning.

### Research and Publications

1. Grants with potential linkage to the faculty's community-based teaching.

2. Professional presentations (on a local, state, or national level) describing community-based teaching or community issues.

3. Publications describing community-based teaching or community issues.

4. Community projects, papers or reports, presentations related to community-based teaching or community issues.

### Service

1. Community projects, papers or reports, presentations related to community-based teaching or community issues.

2. University-related service through community-based teaching and learning that assists the university in addressing community needs.

While it is unlikely that all of these will be evident in any one faculty member's vitae, a global assessment of these measures will assist in developing a profile of faculty roles in the community and the impact of service-learning on faculty scholarship.

## Classroom Observation

### Purpose

The purpose of classroom observation is to describe quantitatively and qualitatively the teaching methods, learning experiences, and interactions that take place in a community-based or service-learning course. Classroom observations can also provide indications of the integration of community focus within the academic content of a course, and descriptions of how and to what extent it is integrated. When used as ongoing data collection in a course, classroom observations can display changes or lack of changes in faculty, student, and community roles, in the course pedagogy, and in the course content. Overall, classroom observations provide a powerful profile of pedagogy and curriculum in service- and community-based learning courses.

In this form of qualitative research, the researcher studies the subject in naturalistic settings, where everyday interactions take place. The natural environment of the subject is important to the qualitative researcher, who gains clues from the context in which the study takes place. Furthermore, this form of qualitative research is descriptive in nature, using words, stories, and metaphors to communicate findings. In observation studies, "human experiences are examined through detailed descriptions of the people being studied" (Creswell, 1994, p. 12).

### Preparation

In preparation for classroom observations, the following sequence of steps is recommended:

1. Observers are trained in observation strategies (training includes practice observations in pairs to establish reliability).

2. An orientation session for faculty is held to introduce the processes to faculty and students, introduce the observer and his/her role, and for completion of human subjects review or other permission forms if necessary.

3. The faculty and observer come to agreement about which class sessions within a semester or quarter will be most representative of "typical" classes, interactions, and content. For example, observation during the showing of a film is not appropriate.

4. Observers review narrative recording format for observation.

### Administration

Observations should be conducted at regular intervals and be well-coordinated with the participating faculty member. An example would be a set of five observations at two-week intervals in a ten-week course during which an entire three-hour period is observed at each observation. The same observer should remain with the class for most of the observations, with the exception of an inter-rater reliability option that may be gained by using a different trained observer for one or two of the sessions.

Using the observation form observers will collect three kinds of primary data:

1. AWARENESS AND INVOLVEMENT OF COMMUNITY: quantity and quality of interactions of community or community partner(s), direct quotations from students and faculty about community, and reference to community integrated in academic content.

2. **TEACHING METHODS:** influence of community-based learning on initial and evolving class format, organization, pedagogy, and faculty/student interactions.

3. **PHILOSOPHY OF TEACHING AND LEARNING:** initial and ongoing faculty/student/community roles, outcomes, pedagogy, curriculum, and interactions.

The classroom observation form (see next page) provides a format for gathering data from observations. Observers often keep their notations in separate journals or notebooks but they should include all of the information deemed necessary to ensure consistency of data collection throughout observations. While the observer should note what is occurring in the classroom as far as content, the bigger picture includes the environment, frequency of interactions between faculty/students and/or community representatives, and daily issues, with regard to service placement and anecdotal information from all constituencies.

Observers are encouraged to keep a journal as their means of reflecting on the process of data collection. While observations are meant to be as objective as possible, observer journals provide insights as to process, and can also serve to clarify issues which may arise during the data analysis.

## Analysis

Classroom observations yield rich and abundant data. The analysis should include the frequency of interactions between students and faculty over a period of time as well as data about changing roles of faculty, students, and community.

The process for analyzing the narrative data from classroom observation requires the same successive readings described in the analysis section for the faculty interview. From the readings key phrases and themes emerge to be later categorized in patterns and in relation to the faculty concepts previously presented.

## Observation Form

Course _____

Date, Day _____

Time _____

Observer _____

# of students _____

Others _____

# of students who spoke _____

Room Arrangement

_____

_____

_____

_____

In the box above, code interactions with an F for faculty and S for students; Use \ to indicate beginning or end of exchange between one or more class participants.

Indicate with an X and record the time spent on the following class activities (format and organization).

Lecture _____     Individual Work _____

Discussion _____     Presentations _____

Group Work _____     Reflection _____

Assessment _____     Question/Answer _____

**Narrative:** Describe the relationships between faculty and students, between students themselves; use of teaching tools (handouts, audiovisual, etc.); mention of community (examples, anecdotes, questions, references, applications); and connections between community experiences and course content. [use multiple pages for narrative]

## Teaching/Learning Continua

### Purpose

The use of the teaching/learning continua helps to describe the teaching/learning context, philosophy, and qualities of the teaching/learning approaches. The right side of each of the continua suggests a high level of interaction is occurring between the faculty and the students, while the left side of each is suggestive of a lower level of exchange between them. The continua offer another lens through which to observe service- or community-based learning courses. They are best used with other observational recording strategies, the observation form previously described, and narrative recordings of individual class sessions.

### Preparation

For purposes of describing recommendations for administration, this section will focus on using the continua only for classroom observations. In preparation for using the continua, the following steps are recommended:

1. Observers are trained in the use of the continua concepts (training includes practice observations in pairs to establish reliability in defining and identifying concepts on the continua).

2. Faculty and observers collaboratively determine which class sessions within the term (semester or quarter) are most representative of the course content and class interactions.

3. Observers schedule the timing of the observations with ample time to complete the continua at the conclusion of each classroom observation.

### Administration

The continua are intended for use at the end of a class session, and are meant to capture the observer's overall impression of the classroom interactions. They are not meant to be analyzed in great detail by the observer. Therefore, the time requirements for completing the continua are minimal but dependent on individual style of reflection (5–15 minutes).

Before training and actual use of the continua, those studying service-learning courses need to engage in discussion of the concepts of the continua and to develop clear and accepted definitions. Examples of classroom practices and situations will be helpful during the discussion. As a starting point, the following definitions and questions for probing the concept are provided.

### Definitions of Teaching/Learning Contexts Used in the Continua

COMMITMENT TO OTHERS: Do the students and faculty seem to be empathetic and/or interested in other people's needs or interests? Do they express a commitment to discovering community needs or interests, or a similar commitment to their peers' needs and interests?

STUDENTS' ROLE: Are the students actively involved in the teaching and learning processes? Do they make decisions about content, processes, etc.?

**FACULTY ROLE:** Is the faculty in a directive role of managing, ordering, instructing? Is there a sense of the faculty "in charge" with authority and control? Or is the faculty in a role of support, assistance, help, collaboration, and making resources available?

**LEARNING ORIENTATION:** Is the learning environment a collective one in which students and faculty work together, and are committed to helping the entire class learn? Or is the learning environment one in which there is more of an individual focus where each individual is directed to their own personal learning?

**PEDAGOGY:** The banking pedagogy refers to a teaching philosophy and process in which a faculty instructor deposits information in students who are expected to respond to occasional withdrawals (exams, etc.). The faculty is the source of information and understandings. The constructivist pedagogy refers to a teaching philosophy and process in which the faculty instructor facilitates experiences in which students construct their own meanings and learning.

## Definitions of Teaching/Learning Qualities Used in the Continua

**THEORY—THEORY & EXPERIENCE:** Does the course rely primarily on established theory or is personal experience coupled and valued with theory for a foundation of course content?

**OTHERS' KNOWLEDGE—PERSONAL KNOWLEDGE:** Is published or expert material the primary and only validated source of information or is personal experience and knowledge also validated as relevant?

**STUDENT AS SPECTATOR—STUDENT AS PARTICIPANT:** Is the student on the sidelines as a passive listener who absorbs the information or is the student playing an active role in the teaching/learning processes?

**FACULTY IN CONTROL—SHARED CONTROL:** Is the faculty in charge and in a position of control of course processes and decisions or do students participate in those processes and decisions?

**STUDENT AS LEARNER—STUDENT AS LEARNER AND TEACHER:** Does the student remain in the traditional role of learner, or does he or she construct course content with the teacher by sharing experiences, raising issues for discussion, and providing information?

**FACULTY AS LEARNER—FACULTY AS TEACHER AND LEARNER:** Does the faculty member remain in the traditional role of teacher, or does he or she share the construction of course content with the students and encourage student directed teaching, consequently becoming learners themselves?

**INDIVIDUAL LEARNING—COLLECTIVE LEARNING:** Are the learning processes focused on each individual being directed to his/her own learning, or is the environment a collective one, with all committed to helping the class as a whole understand the course content?

**DISTINCTION CLEAR BETWEEN TEACHER AND LEARNER—DISTINCTION BLURRED BETWEEN TEACHER AND LEARNER:** Are the roles of the teacher and students distinctive and separate, or do teacher and students trade roles and move in and out of roles during the class sessions?

ANSWERS—QUESTIONS AND ANSWERS: Is course material addressed in such a way that right answers are valued and content presented with certainty of information, or is material presented with issues and questions valued along with answers?

CERTAINTY OF OUTCOMES—UNCERTAINTY OF OUTCOMES: Are there defined, inflexible outcomes for students, or are the outcomes flexible enough to be constructed and revised according to students' needs and interests?

COMMON LEARNING OUTCOMES—INDIVIDUALIZED LEARNING OUTCOMES: Are the outcomes restricted to those set in advance or planned by the group as common for all students, or are the students afforded the opportunity to explore personal learning outcomes?

IGNORANCE AVOIDED—IGNORANCE A RESOURCE: Are questions and misunderstandings treated as a diversion from scheduled class content, or are they treated as an opportunity for new directions or potential for different understandings?

FOCUS-STUDENT NEEDS—FOCUS-STUDENT AND COMMUNITY NEEDS: Is the community service focused on student needs with respect to learning and interests, or are student needs and community needs considered and attended to equally?

## Analysis

The best way to analyze the data from the teaching/learning continua is to use an empty continuum form as a tally sheet for each individual faculty. For each concept, the dates of observations are placed in the appropriate place on each line to indicate the observed qualities or contextual descriptors. The finished tally sheet provides a visual of the course, and of changes or lack of change. For a group of faculty, the individual placements on the lines can be collapsed to the mean or middle placement and then represented in a bar graph for each of the continua's concepts. The data can also be shown for beginning of courses, mid-way points in courses, and end of courses to capture change or lack of change for a group of faculty.

## Continuum of Teaching/Learning Contexts

Circle the X on each continuum below the descriptions that best indicates how you would describe the teaching/learning context of the observed class.

| Commitment to Others | LOW | | | | HIGH |
|---|---|---|---|---|---|
| | 1 | 2 | 3 | 4 | 5 |

| Students' Role | PASSIVE | | | | ACTIVE |
|---|---|---|---|---|---|
| | 1 | 2 | 3 | 4 | 5 |

| Faculty Role | DIRECTIVE | | | | FACILITATIVE |
|---|---|---|---|---|---|
| | 1 | 2 | 3 | 4 | 5 |

| Learning Orientation | INDIVIDUAL | | | | COLLECTIVE |
|---|---|---|---|---|---|
| | 1 | 2 | 3 | 4 | 5 |

| Pedagogy | "BANKING" | | | | CONSTRUCTIVIST |
|---|---|---|---|---|---|
| | 1 | 2 | 3 | 4 | 5 |

Adapted from the work of Jeffrey Howard, University of Michigan (1995)

## Continuum of Teaching/Learning Qualities

Place an X on each continuum to indicate how you would describe the observed class.

THEORY | THEORY & EXPERIENCE
1_____ 2 _____ 3_____ 4 _____ 5

OTHERS' KNOWLEDGE | PERSONAL KNOWLEDGE
1_____ 2 _____ 3_____ 4 _____ 5

STUDENT AS SPECTATOR | STUDENT AS PARTICIPANT
1_____ 2 _____ 3_____ 4 _____ 5

FACULTY IN CONTROL | SHARED CONTROL
1_____ 2 _____ 3_____ 4 _____ 5

STUDENT AS LEARNER | STUDENT AS LEARNER & TEACHER
1_____ 2 _____ 3_____ 4 _____ 5

FACULTY AS TEACHER | FACULTY AS TEACHER & LEARNER
1_____ 2 _____ 3_____ 4 _____ 5

INDIVIDUAL LEARNING | COLLECTIVE LEARNING
1_____ 2 _____ 3_____ 4 _____ 5

DISTINCTION CLEAR B/W | DISTINCTION BLURRED B/W
TEACHER & LEARNER | TEACHER & LEARNER
1_____ 2 _____ 3_____ 4 _____ 5

ANSWERS | QUESTIONS AND ANSWERS
1_____ 2 _____ 3_____ 4 _____ 5

CERTAINTY OF OUTCOMES | UNCERTAINTY OF OUTCOMES
1_____ 2 _____ 3_____ 4 _____ 5

COMMON LEARNING OUTCOMES | INDIVIDUALIZED LEARNING OUTCOMES
1_____ 2 _____ 3_____ 4 _____ 5

IGNORANCE AVOIDED | IGNORANCE A RESOURCE
1_____ 2 _____ 3_____ 4 _____ 5

FOCUS-STUDENT NEEDS | FOCUS-STUDENT/COMMUNITY NEEDS
1_____ 2 _____ 3_____ 4 _____ 5

Adapted from the work of Jeffrey Howard, University of Michigan (1995)

## Faculty Survey

### Purpose

The faculty survey is intended to describe faculty members' perspectives, motivations, concerns, and attitudes on issues related to their experience teaching a service-learning course. The survey is based on a five point Likert scale where faculty report their level of agreement regarding their service-learning course(s). The scale range includes "strongly disagree," "disagree," "neutral," "agree," and "strongly agree." Topics assessed by the survey include faculty's attitude about service, community, and service-learning, the impact they perceive that service-learning has on their students and their scholarly work, and their motivation for incorporating service-learning into their courses. The faculty survey was developed through a process of literature review, survey of existing instruments, and discussions with faculty.

The information gained through the faculty survey is useful for purposes of planning faculty development programs and for attracting and recruiting faculty for service-learning or community-based learning courses. The instrument provides descriptions of various perspectives and experiences of faculty who incorporate service in their academic courses. These descriptions will yield understanding for planning and coordinating campus programs.

In addition to assessing faculty attitudes and perspectives, the faculty survey probes the impact of service-learning on faculty. The survey includes questions pertaining to the influence that service-learning has on a faculty member's community involvement, teaching, and scholarship. These data are useful for assessing the impact of service-learning on both individual faculty and on the institution in general.

As with the student section, two surveys for faculty are presented — one a longer version, and the second a shorter version that can be scanned by institutional research resources for rapid reporting.

### Preparation

Before administering the faculty survey the following preparation steps are recommended.

1. Determine the purpose of instrument use. The decisions include determining if the instrument is to be used in a pre-post assessment of change or in a post-test only approach to describe the general attitudes and perceptions of faculty after they have taught a service-learning course.

2. Consider using other data-gathering strategies to complement use of the faculty survey to develop a more complete and useful profile of faculty perspectives and attitudes. This instrument is ideally used prior to conducting faculty interviews. Faculty syllabi and teaching materials will be useful additions to the data from the faculty survey. To gain a full picture of a course, the faculty survey will complement data yielded by the student surveys.

3. Determine appropriate scheduling of the instrument use. Schedule the administration of the survey in consideration of faculty time and convenience.

4. Solicit faculty consent and support for the instrument use. Well in advance of using the faculty survey, faculty should be informed of its purpose and their consent obtained, preferably in writing.

## Administration

Once the preparation steps are complete, the following administration procedures are recommended for use of the faculty survey.

1. Faculty anonymity should be assured to them and maintained throughout the collection of data from the survey.

2. Faculty should be informed that the instrument will take 15–20 minutes to complete.

3. If the instrument is mailed to faculty, clear information should be included about returning the survey (timing and where to return the form).

## Analysis

Data analysis can be conducted through utilization of the Statistical Package for Social Sciences (SPSS) software. In the case of assessing and comparing pre- and post-service-learning experiences, the analysis could include frequencies, descriptive statistics, Chi-squares, Analyses of Variance (ANOVA), and factor analysis. First, descriptive statistics and frequencies serve as a database, providing mean, mode, and standard deviation between items. Second, Chi-squares correlate demographic data between faculty. Third, Factor Analysis reduces items into categories that are closely related. Finally, ANOVA's are useful to explore the existence of variation between faculty on either single items or groups of items that may arise from the factor analysis.

## Community-Based Learning—Faculty Survey

We would like to better understand the impact that community-based learning has on faculty. Please assist us by responding to the following questions.

I. **First, we would like to know some information about you.**

1. How long have you been teaching at a postsecondary level?_____

2. Was this your first community-based learning course?_____

3. The course number and title you taught: _____

II. **We would like to gain your perspective about this community-based learning course.**
*Please indicate your level of agreement with each statement.*

| | Strongly Disagree | Disagree | Neutral | Agree | Strongly Agree |
|---|---|---|---|---|---|
| 4. The community participation aspect of this course helped students to see how the subject matter they learned can be used in everyday life. | ❑ | ❑ | ❑ | ❑ | ❑ |
| 5. The community work in this course helped students to better understand the lectures and readings in this class. | ❑ | ❑ | ❑ | ❑ | ❑ |
| 6. I feel that students would have learned more from this course if more time had been spent in the classroom instead of doing community work. | ❑ | ❑ | ❑ | ❑ | ❑ |
| 7. The idea of combining work in the community with university coursework should be practiced in more courses at this university. | ❑ | ❑ | ❑ | ❑ | ❑ |

III. **The next set of questions relates to your attitude toward community involvement.**

| | Strongly Disagree | Disagree | Neutral | Agree | Strongly Agree |
|---|---|---|---|---|---|
| 8. I was already volunteering in my community before this course. | ❑ | ❑ | ❑ | ❑ | ❑ |
| 9. The community participation aspect of this course showed me how I can become more involved in my community. | ❑ | ❑ | ❑ | ❑ | ❑ |

| | Strongly Disagree | Disagree | Neutral | Agree | Strongly Agree |
|---|---|---|---|---|---|
| 10. I feel that the community work being done through this class benefited the community. | ❑ | ❑ | ❑ | ❑ | ❑ |
| 11. I probably won't volunteer or participate in the community now that this class is finished. | ❑ | ❑ | ❑ | ❑ | ❑ |
| 12. The community work involved in this course helped me to become more aware of the needs in my community. | ❑ | ❑ | ❑ | ❑ | ❑ |
| 13. I have a responsibility to serve my community. | ❑ | ❑ | ❑ | ❑ | ❑ |

**IV. Next, we would like to know the influence of your service on your professional development.**

| | Strongly Disagree | Disagree | Neutral | Agree | Strongly Agree |
|---|---|---|---|---|---|
| 14. Doing work in the community helped me to define my personal strengths and weaknesses. | ❑ | ❑ | ❑ | ❑ | ❑ |
| 15. Performing work in the community helped me clarify areas of focus for my scholarship. | ❑ | ❑ | ❑ | ❑ | ❑ |
| 16. Teaching a community-based learning course resulted in a change in my teaching orientation. | ❑ | ❑ | ❑ | ❑ | ❑ |
| 17. This community-based learning course is an important entry in my portfolio. | ❑ | ❑ | ❑ | ❑ | ❑ |

**V. Next, we would like some of your personal reflections on this experience.**

| | Strongly Disagree | Disagree | Neutral | Agree | Strongly Agree |
|---|---|---|---|---|---|
| 18. Most people can make a difference in their community. | ❑ | ❑ | ❑ | ❑ | ❑ |
| 19. I was able to develop a good relationship with the students in this course because of the community work we performed. | ❑ | ❑ | ❑ | ❑ | ❑ |
| 20. I was comfortable working with cultures other than my own. | ❑ | ❑ | ❑ | ❑ | ❑ |

| | Strongly Disagree | Disagree | Neutral | Agree | Strongly Agree |
|---|---|---|---|---|---|
| 21. The community work involved in this course made me aware of some of my own biases and prejudices. | ❑ | ❑ | ❑ | ❑ | ❑ |
| 22. Participating in the community helped me enhance my leadership skills. | ❑ | ❑ | ❑ | ❑ | ❑ |
| 23. The work we performed in the community enhanced my ability to communicate my ideas in a real world context. | ❑ | ❑ | ❑ | ❑ | ❑ |
| 24. I can make a difference in my community. | ❑ | ❑ | ❑ | ❑ | ❑ |

VI.  **Finally, please answer some questions about the process of teaching a community-based course.**

25. What was (were) your reason(s) for deciding to teach a community-based learning course? *Please indicate all reasons that apply and rank them in order of importance (1 being most important).*

Need to try something new _____
Desire for increased relevance in courses _____
Encouragement from colleagues _____
Resources ($) to support the course _____
Faculty incentive money _____
Have taught these courses before _____
For professional recognition _____
Curiosity _____
Other: _____ _____

26. How did you handle the logistics of your community-based learning course? *Please check the most accurate response.*

I made the arrangements and placements. _____

A graduate student who works with me made the arrangements and placements. _____

The graduate student and I worked together on the arrangements and placements. _____

Students handled their own placements. _____

The community representative handled the arrangements and placements. _____

Other: _____ _____

27. Now that this course is completed, my most serious concern about teaching a community-based learning course is:
*Please indicate all responses that apply and rank them in order of importance (1 being most important).*

Time constraints _____

Coordination of placements _____

Supervision of students _____

Communication with community representative(s) _____

Reduced time for classroom instruction _____

Unpredictable nature of community work _____

Assessment of students' learning and work _____

Costs _____

Other: _____ _____

28. Teaching a community-based learning course has had an impact on the following:
*Please indicate all responses that apply and rank them in order of importance (1 being most important).*

My research agenda _____

My plans for publications and presentations
  (scholarly work) _____

Other classes I teach _____

My own personal service in the community _____

My relationships with faculty colleagues _____

My relationships with students _____

My relationships with community partners _____

Other: _____ _____

Finally, please add any other comments you have about teaching courses where learning takes place in a community setting. *(Please use the space below or attach an additional sheet of paper.)*

*Thank you for your insights regarding community-based learning!*

## Community-Based Learning — Faculty Survey

We would like to better understand the impact that community-based learning has on faculty. Please assist us by taking 5 –10 minutes to complete this survey, and return it to [directions personalized to institution].

### I. First we would like some information about you.

1. How long have you been teaching at the postsecondary level? _____ [number of years]

2. Approximately how many times have you taught community-based learning courses?
   ❑ Once          ❑ 2-5          ❑ 6-10          ❑ More than 10

3. Are there other faculty in your department/program teaching community-based learning courses?
   ❑ Yes                    ❑ No

4. What is the academic level of the students in this community-based learning course?
   ❑ Freshmen          ❑ Sophomore          ❑ Junior
   ❑ Senior          ❑ Capstone          ❑ Graduate

### II. Next we would like to gain your perspective about this community-based learning course.

5. Mark the place on each of the four scales below to indicate how you would describe the student and faculty roles in the community-based classroom experience.

| | | | | | | |
|---|---|---|---|---|---|---|
| Student as learner | ❑ | ❑ | ❑ | ❑ | ❑ | Student as learner & teacher |
| Student as spectator | ❑ | ❑ | ❑ | ❑ | ❑ | Student as participant |
| Faculty in control | ❑ | ❑ | ❑ | ❑ | ❑ | Shared control |
| Faculty as teacher | ❑ | ❑ | ❑ | ❑ | ❑ | Faculty as teacher & learner |

### III. The next set of questions relates to your experience and concept of community involvement.

| | Strongly Agree | Agree | Neutral | Disgree | Strongly Disagree |
|---|---|---|---|---|---|
| 6. I had previous community volunteer experience prior to teaching my first community-based learning course. | ❑ | ❑ | ❑ | ❑ | ❑ |
| 7. I believe that the community work done through this class has benefited the community. | ❑ | ❑ | ❑ | ❑ | ❑ |
| 8. I will volunteer or participate in the community now that this class has finished. | ❑ | ❑ | ❑ | ❑ | ❑ |

| | Strongly Agree | Agree | Neutral | Disgree | Strongly Disagree |
|---|---|---|---|---|---|
| 9. The community work involved in this course has deepened my understanding of community needs. | ❏ | ❏ | ❏ | ❏ | ❏ |
| 10. I believe that as a faculty member I have a responsibility to serve my community. | ❏ | ❏ | ❏ | ❏ | ❏ |

**IV. Next we would like to know the influence of your service on your personal and professional development.** *Please indicate your level of agreement with each of the following statements.*

| | Strongly Agree | Agree | Neutral | Disgree | Strongly Disagree |
|---|---|---|---|---|---|
| 11. Performing work in the community has helped me to focus on specific areas for my scholarship. | ❏ | ❏ | ❏ | ❏ | ❏ |
| 12. Teaching a community-based learning course has resulted in a change in my teaching strategies. | ❏ | ❏ | ❏ | ❏ | ❏ |
| 13. I found that my relationship with the students was enhanced because of the community work we performed. | ❏ | ❏ | ❏ | ❏ | ❏ |
| 14. Participating in the community has helped me enhance my leadership skills. | ❏ | ❏ | ❏ | ❏ | ❏ |

*Please add any other comments you may have.*

**V. Finally we would like you to comment on future community-based learning courses.**

15. Now that this course is finished, you may still have concerns about teaching community-based learning course. Please mark any of the following that are concerns of yours.
   ❏ Time constraints      ❏ Communication with community representative(s)
   ❏ Coordination of placements      ❏ Reduced time for classroom instruction
   ❏ Supervision of students      ❏ Unpredictable nature of community work
   ❏ Assessment of students' learning      ❏ Costs
   ❏ Other (please specify) _____

16. Reflecting back on this community-based learning experience, what ideas do you have for your next community-based learning class to improve the overall experience for you, your students, and the community partners?

*Thank you for your comments.*
*Please return this by [insert date] to [insert relevant mailing address].*

# Community Impact

## Why Assess Impact on the Community?

Service-learning is impossible without community involvement. Effective and sustainable service-learning depends on mutually-beneficial partnerships between campus and community (Holland & Gelmon, 1998). Yet much assessment work, prior to our initial work at Portland State University, focused almost exclusively on assessment of impact on students. The goals of our assessment project included understanding multiple impacts and gathering information to improve service-learning. Thus, it was essential to assess community as a distinct constituency. But how does one define community? There is no one "community." In fact, early on in our work we asked faculty to define their perceptions of "who is the community" and we received a wide variety of answers. Developing an understanding of perceptions of community and what that means to students, faculty, and the institution, let alone the community partner, is therefore essential.

For our work we focused primarily on the community partner organization that participated in the service-learning experience for each individual course (recognizing that in some courses there were multiple community partners). Given the importance of the partner organization to the service-learning opportunity and experience, the focus of assessment was on impacts on their organization and their perception of the service-learning project. We looked to the partner organization to give us feedback regarding any impact on clients, not being so presumptuous as to try to make causal relationships between the work students did and changes in, for example, clients' health status, emotional well-being, job security, or housing stability. Clearly these indicators might be valuable information for the partner to have, but we did not feel they were relevant measures to focus on, given our goal of understanding the community-university collaboration and partnership that underlies service-learning programs.

Service-learning is intensive and demanding work for community partners. Most important to our assessment was to understand partner perceptions of the impact of service-learning on their operations so we could identify needed improvements and ensure reciprocity.

## Understanding Assessment of Impact on Community

Talking about "community" implies that the community is a single entity, a unitary concept, and a definable organization. In fact, issues addressed by students through a community-based learning experience are part of a much larger system that includes residents, government, law enforcement, business, housing, schools, health and social services, and economic development (Scholtes, 1997). Individuals who work in, interact with, or produce materials for these various sectors bring different perspectives and varying views of the sources of problems and potential solutions (Knapp et al., 2000). Efforts to take all of these perspectives into account in trying to assess impact on community may be formidable, and might create overwhelming barriers to completion of assessment.

In a review of research on community as a key factor in service-learning, Cruz and Giles (2000) identify political, intellectual, and practical dimensions as obstacles to research on the community focus in the service-learning literature. The political concern relates to questions about academic rigor in studying the community; the intellectual focuses on an inability to define community and therefore to define appropriate methodologies to study it; and the practical addresses the lack of resources and knowledge to pursue this line of inquiry. They reach three conclusions about community and service-learning as supported by the literature:

- service-learning contributes to community development

- service-learning bridges town-gown gaps

- service-learning offers benefits to community partners

In addition to these conclusions, there is also the issue of community interests in student preparation. Partners see service-learning as a tool to attract students to civic service or to non-profit careers — or at least to help students become "citizen professionals." Understanding this interest of the community partners is another important element of assessing impact from a community perspective.

One of the challenges faced by universities when working with communities is that there is often a chasm between the (unrealized) expectations and (mis)understandings of the community partners and the services/resources the university can provide (Wealthall et al., 1998). A significant area of focus, therefore, for the university is to pay special attention to clarifying abilities and expectations, and to ensure that students and faculty work closely with community liaisons to develop genuine understandings of each other's context and perspectives, and the ability to respond to assets and needs. Inevitably, community need is far greater than the capacity of the campus service-learning effort (Gelmon, Holland, et al., 1998b). The assessment challenge lies in clarifying what is reasonable to expect and accomplish within the service-learning activity, determining to what extent this has been accomplished, and gaining understanding of the barriers and facilitators of these accomplishments. Thus the unit of analysis is the partnership relationship itself, as well as the partner organization's perceptions of impact.

Assessment of community involvement in service-learning raises issues about methodologies that have not been answered to date (Gelmon, 2000a). Is there a difference in assessing the impact on the community as compared to the impact on the community-university partnership? One must be able to define the community component relevant to the assessment, and then describe the elements of the partnership. One useful approach from which to build assessment of partnership relationships could be to rely upon the "Principles of Partnership" articulated by Community-Campus Partnerships for Health (CCPH). These principles are one of the few examples in the public domain today, and they work well for partnerships across the higher education spectrum, even though they were initially articulated in the context of health professions education (Seifer & Maurana, 2000). These principles are:

1. Partners have agreed upon mission, values, goals, and measurable outcomes for the partnership.

2. The relationship between partners is characterized by mutual trust, respect, genuineness, and commitment.

3. The partnership builds upon identified strengths and assets, but also addresses areas that need improvement.

4. The partnership balances the power among partners and enables resources among partners to be shared.

5. There is clear, open, and accessible communication between partners, making it an on-going priority to listen to each need, develop a common language, and validate/clarify the meaning of terms.

6. Roles, norms, and processes for the partnership are established with the input and agreement of all partners.

7. There is feedback to, among, and from all stakeholders in the partnership, with the goal of continuously improving the partnership and its outcomes.

8. Partners share the credit for the partnership's accomplishments.

9. Partnerships take time to develop and evolve over time.

A set of key factors for successful student/community partnership projects, identified through an educational collaborative addressing community health improvement (Knapp et al., 2000), offers another useful approach for thinking about assessment of community impact. The original factors, which focused specifically on health issues, have been edited to have broader relevance for a number of disciplines in higher education:

- All members of the partnership must understand the community issues and ensure there is relevant community data available prior to student involvement.

- Connect the institution and the community, so that faculty have knowledge of the community and the issues being addressed, and can facilitate the connections between the students and the community, and so that community representatives have knowledge of the academic institution and the issues being addressed in the service-learning activity.

- Jointly define target populations so that student projects focus on specific groups rather than the entire community.

- Members of the partnership understand the people to be served, and design and implement appropriate, client-sensitive approaches.

- Partners work together to identify appropriate, short-term projects that are doable in the time students have and contribute to the knowledge base of both the community organization and the students.

- The partnership members practice and model interdisciplinary teamwork, since community issues and actions are intrinsically interdisciplinary.

These factors clearly would contribute to design of service-learning experiences, but could also then form the basis for articulating the focus of the assessment. While the emphasis here is on understanding community impact, the focus of each factor shows the inter-relationship of student, faculty, and institutional perspectives with those of the community. These factors can in turn be linked to core concepts for understanding impact of service-learning on the community, and impact of the community on service-learning.

Another approach that includes attention to learning is offered by Holland (2000b). She offers the following characteristics of sustainable partnerships that could serve as a framework for assessment:

- joint exploration of separate and common goals and interests

- creation of a mutually rewarding shared agenda

- articulation of clear consequences for each partner

- success measured in both institutional and community terms

- shared control of partnership directions and/or resources

- effective use and enhancement of community capacity

- identification of opportunities for early success and regular celebration

- focus on knowledge exchange, shared two-way learning and capacity building

- attention to communication and open cultivation of trust

- commitment to continuous assessment of the partnership itself, as well as to outcomes

Assessment of community impact can also develop from theories and concepts of community development and community-building. In addition to adopting an "assets" rather than "needs" approach (Kretzman & McKnight, 1993), community-building frameworks may offer insights into leadership, knowledge, creativity, and problem-solving capacities (Keith, 1998). There is little, if any, documented assessment literature using such frameworks, suggesting an opportunity for service-learning educators to team up with their colleagues in community development to more explicitly articulate methods for this area of assessment.

Some examples of models of assessment of community impact exist in the literature. The assessment of the impact of service-learning in health professions education, through a national demonstration program known as Health Professions Schools in Service to the Nation, incorporated one research question addressing impact on community-university partnerships, and another question addressing impact on the partners themselves (Gelmon, Holland et al., 1998a and 1998b). Some foundations have reported assessments aimed at understanding the impact of social intervention programs on community change (Annie E. Casey Foundation, 1999; Connell et al., 1995; Petersen, 1998). Early evidence about the use of a model being referred to as the "3-I Model" (initiator, initiative, impact) suggests potential assessment applications for understanding community change (Clarke, 2000).

Future work on assessment of community impact may be aided by the approach recommended by Cruz and Giles (2000). They suggest 1) using the community-university partnership as the unit of analysis (Seifer & Maurana, 2000); 2) giving serious attention to the principles of good practice for service-learning (Sigmon, 1979; Honnet & Poulsen, 1989) regarding community input, reciprocity, and partnership; 3) using action research (Harkavy, Puckett, & Romer, 2000); and 4) focusing on an assets-based approach (Kretzman & McKnight, 1993). The assessment model presented here incorporates elements of all four strategies. It is unique in terms of the deference it gives to the community partners and the importance of their articulation and interpretation of any impact. Partnerships must be assessed as part of the overall assessment of the impact of service-learning.

## Assessment Matrix for Community

An assessment matrix for understanding the community constituency is presented in Table 7. This matrix is based upon experiences in several programs and is presented as a synthesis of best practices based upon those evaluations (Driscoll et al., 1998; Shinnamon, Gelmon, & Holland, 1999; Gelmon, McBride, et al., 1999). The concepts (variables) are presented in two sections: those most applicable to the community partner organization itself, and those related to the community-university partnership.

In considering those concepts related to the community partner organization, individuals designing the assessment must be cautious to avoid identifying concepts that might be interpreted as part of a performance review of the organization. Such a review must not be the focus in assessing impact of service-learning, but there may be concepts that are appealing to the university participants but would be viewed as threatening or intrusive by the community partner. Thus, the three concepts presented focus explicitly on how the participation of the partner organization in the academic activity affects the partner. Based upon our experiences, there are three main areas on which to focus:

**Capacity to fulfill organizational mission:** The service-learning activity may affect the types of services offered, the number of clients served, and the variety of activities offered. The number of students who can be accommodated by the organization might also change, and have a relationship to capacity. Organizations that are primarily volunteer-driven are able to increase their organizational capacity significantly through service-learning partnerships. Finally, through its interaction with university representatives, the organization may gain insights into assets and needs (of itself, its clients, or the university) that may affect organizational capacity or program strategies.

**Economic benefits:** Through the participation of faculty and students in the service-learning interaction, organizations may derive economic benefits or cost burdens in terms of resource utilization (human, fiscal, information, or physical resources). Sometimes organizations identify new staff (generally from among the student participants), and are spared the time and expense of a costly search process. The community-university collaboration may also facilitate identification of new funding opportunities for which the community organization may apply (with or without the participation of the university), thus again contributing to economic benefits. Another benefit is the completion of projects with the addition of new expertise that the organization might not normally have readily available (e.g., graphic design, diversity training, development of marketing materials). Such benefits are often one of the motivators for community organizations to partner with academic institutions.

**Social benefits:** Through the collaboration with the university, the community organization may identify new connections or networks — sometimes with individuals, and sometimes with other community organizations (particularly if the university brings together multiple community partners in community advisory committees or through other cross-organization collaborations). Organizations also often report an increase in number of volunteers, when students continue their involvement after the academic project (and often bring their friends and families to the volunteer experience). There may also be an impact on community issues (such as neighborhood policing, improved lighting, lead abatement, accessible immunization clinics) as a result of the service-learning activity, again offering social benefit for the organization and its community. Assessment can help community partners to think about new and sometimes better ways to work with volunteers in general (not just students).

The second set of concepts relates to the community-university partnership itself. There are challenges to this aspect of assessment because of the somewhat intangible nature of partnerships, and the difficulties in defining what can be assessed. As a result, some of these concepts reflect documentable indicators, and others relate to the processes that support and contribute to the partnership.

**Nature of community-university relationship (partnership):** The core of this concept is a description of the process by which partnerships are established. This is illustrated by gaining the partners' perspectives on the kinds of activities conducted, and of the barriers and facilitators to both establishing the partnership and engaging in these activities. Investigation of the nature of partnerships can reveal important insights about mutual respect and common goals, and can highlight many of the components cited in the various principles/characteristics of partnerships (Seifer & Maurana, 2000; Knapp et al., 2000; Holland, 2000b).

**Nature of community-university interaction:** A core element of partnerships is the nature and kind of interactions that take place — and ideally there are multiple interactions, rather than simply the act of students going to the partner organization and working on a specific activity. Interactions may be seen where community partners go to campus to participate (in classroom-based reflection sessions, or in program planning activities for example), and where campus representatives go to the community organization (to attend community advisory group meetings, to volunteer, or to participate in community activities). The partnership might also focus on very specific work, such as web design, multi-media presentation development, or brochure production. Communication is an essential element of the partnership, and attention should be given to the methods and patterns of communication. Finally, interactions can be understood through description of levels of awareness the partners have about each other's programs and activities.

**Satisfaction with partnership:** Satisfaction is essential to the development, implementation, and maintenance of a partnership. The key elements here are the perceptions of mutuality of effort and reciprocity in activity (Gelmon, Holland, and Shinnamon, 1998). The assessment of this concept requires creation of a safe environment in which participants in the partnership can offer praise as well as express concerns without fear of reprisal. Cultural norms regarding expression of satisfaction must be taken into account when attempting to collect data on this concept. Another element of satisfaction can be assessed through understanding of responsiveness to concerns — again, responsiveness by all participants in the partnership. Assessments must be designed to take into account these multiple perspectives (and avoid falling into the trap of only considering the university's perspective). This concept offers considerable opportunity for unanticipated findings regarding sources of satisfaction.

**Sustainability of partnership:** Significant effort is invested in creating partnerships and, if they are successful, there is usually a desire to sustain these efforts. Sustainability can be understood through gaining insights into the duration of partnerships and the evolution they go through. In particular, identification of key events throughout the partnership that created barriers to collaboration or accelerated collaborative efforts can provide useful insights into the strengths and benefits of the partnership. In assessing sustainability, it is essential to try to understand the partners' intention in sustaining a relationship, and to investigate both the time invested to build the partnership and to maintain it over time. As well, insights can be gathered into how the partners recognize if the partnership is not meeting their goals.

## Strategies for Assessing Impact on Community

A key issue in engaging the community partner in assessment is to be respectful of their time, obligations, and resources. Students can be required to spend a substantial amount of time writing a reflective journal, but one cannot expect that commitment of community partners. Similarly, faculty can be expected to convene at the researcher's convenience for interviews or focus groups, but the researcher must go to the community partner for an interview (at the partner's convenience). There must also be sufficient benefits offered for community partners to come together at a central location during peak working hours for a focus group. Careful attention must be given to selecting methods for assessment of community impact that create the least burden of evaluation and provide the most benefit for the university and the community partner. This may result in some compromises in terms of the kinds of data that can be collected, but this will be offset by the increased responsiveness and enhanced quality of data contributed.

Community partners value the opportunity to provide feedback, and often report that the invitations to participate in assessment activities help them to feel that their role in the university's activities is a valued one. Partners are sometimes intimidated by participating in university discussions if they themselves do not have the academic credentials evident among faculty and institutional administrators. Such concerns need to be carefully addressed, so that partners do feel welcome and appreciated.

A distinct challenge is to create the appropriate communication environment where community partners feel able to speak candidly about experiences, offering praise but also sharing critical and/or reflective observations. Partners are usually eager to praise, in particular because they are often grateful for the service provided and the benefits they derive from the partnership. Some partners, however, are reluctant to be critical for fear of "retribution" and potentially losing the partnership or jeopardizing their relationship with the faculty member. There may also be cultural norms about not criticizing someone who is helping you. Attention must be given to encouraging candid feedback from the partners with the emphasis on improving the work done together, and with adequate assurances that criticism will not lead to any negative actions.

One of the particular benefits accrued from incorporating a community voice is to gain an additional perspective from outside the university. Community partners can offer incredibly valuable insights about, for example, student preparation for the service experience that may either validate or obviate what the faculty member has reported about how they have prepared the students. Similarly, students may report their perceptions about the value of their service, and these may again be similar or opposite to the perceptions the community partner has of the value of their contribution. This should not be interpreted as suggesting that the students and faculty are always positive, and the community partner opinion is always contradictory; sometimes the community partner expresses much greater satisfaction than either students or faculty have observed! Observations of students in community settings help to highlight the benefits and challenges present in these relationships, and may also highlight areas where changes are needed in activity design, communications, or other areas of interaction.

Specific comments regarding the various methods offered for assessment of community impact are similar to those found in preceding sections for the specific techniques. Thus the reader is referred to the previous discussions of strategies for assessment to gain insights regarding methods such as surveys, focus groups, and interviews. A few particular observations are noted below.

**Community partner survey:** Faculty need to be contacted early in the academic term in order for the researcher to obtain the contact information for each partner. Faculty must also be assured that their community partner information is confidential and will not be shared (unless they have no objections); some faculty are concerned about "losing" their partner. A copy of the survey should be shared with the faculty so they know what questions are being asked of the partner.

**Community observation:** While this can provide rich data, it may be logistically difficult to organize. Sometimes observations are viewed as intrusive, and care should be taken to avoid this. Such difficulties are offset, however, by the opportunity to better understand the context in which students are working, in particular with respect to logistics, communication, and the relevance of the course project to agency activities. The contact made during an observation may also facilitate community partner responsiveness to a subsequent survey or a request for an interview or focus group participation.

**Community focus group:** Focus groups of community partners can be difficult to organize in terms of finding a time that is convenient. Convening the focus group over a meal and on campus — perhaps in conjunction with a campus tour if these are new partners — can help to entice partners to attend. One of the side benefits of a focus group of partners is the additional networking that may occur among the partners — those who already have relationships, and those who are meeting other community members for the first time. Hosting a focus group on campus helps the university to convey its appreciation to the partners, particularly if the group meets in an environment that is welcoming.

**Community partner interview:** Interviews of community partners may be threatening to faculty, so care should be taken to ensure that faculty understand the content of the interview protocol and the purpose of the interview itself. Interviews also take time, which is a commodity that many partners feel is lacking; however, some partners may prefer an interview at their site rather than having to travel to participate in a focus group. Thus the interview must be very focused in order to obtain maximum benefit for the institution, the faculty member, and the partner. The interview can provide valuable information to understand the complexity of partnerships, and allows the community partner to express the extent to which they feel a part of the educational process. A benefit of the interview can be to convey to the partner that their relationship with the university has the potential to go beyond one course and one faculty member, if they wish and it is appropriate. They may identify other opportunities for student and faculty involvement in their organization as a result of the interview.

## Concluding Thoughts

The community presents perhaps the most challenging aspect of assessment of the impact of service-learning for two main reasons. First, as described previously, it is difficult to define what we mean by "community" and researchers must clearly embrace a definition that articulates what aspects of organization, clients, and larger social systems will be included in the assessment. Second, the community is its own agent, and not under the oversight of the university, so the ability to require participation in assessment and link it to any sort of rewards or punishments is negligible. Thus the researchers face the challenge of creating an assessment plan which will get community partner buy-in — in terms of methods, time commitment, and potential benefit of the results.

Despite these two challenges, insights from the community partners and about community-university partnerships provide rich and essential information for understanding the overall impact of service-learning. The next pages present examples of assessment methods for understanding community impact.

## Table 7: Matrix for Community Assessment

| What do we want to know? (concepts) | How will we know it? (indicators) | How will we measure it? (methods) | Who/what will provide the data? (sources) |
|---|---|---|---|
| **Variables about community partner organization** | | | |
| Capacity to fulfill organizational mission | Types of services provided<br>Number of clients served<br>Number of students involved<br>Variety of activities offered<br>Insights into assets and needs | Survey<br>Interview<br>Focus groups<br>Documentation review<br>Critical incident review | Community partner<br>Students<br>Faculty<br>Advisory committees<br>Governing board |
| Economic benefits | Identification of new staff<br>Impact on resource utilization through services provided by faculty/students<br>Identification of funding opportunities | Interview<br>Focus groups<br>Documentation review | Community partner<br>Students<br>Faculty<br>Governing board |
| Social benefits | New connections or networks<br>Number of volunteers<br>Impact on community issues | Interview<br>Focus groups<br>Documentation review | Community partner<br>Students<br>Faculty<br>Governing board |
| **Variables about community-university partnership** | | | |
| Nature of community-university relationship (partnership) | Creation of partnerships<br>Kinds of activities conducted<br>Barriers/facilitators | Interview<br>Critical incident review<br>Documentation review | Community partner<br>Faculty<br>Governing board |
| Nature of community-university interaction | Involvement in each others' activities<br>Communication patterns<br>Community awareness of university programs and activities<br>University awareness of community programs and activities | Interview<br>Focus groups<br>Documentation review | Community partner<br>Faculty<br>Students<br>Advisory committees |
| Satisfaction with partnership | Perception of mutuality and reciprocity<br>Responsiveness to concerns<br>Willingness to provide feedback | Interview<br>Survey<br>Focus group | Community partner<br>Faculty<br>Governing board |
| Sustainability of partnership | Duration<br>Evolution | Interview<br>Survey<br>Critical incident review | Community partner<br>Faculty<br>Governing board |

# Strategies and Methods: Community

## Community Observation

### Purpose

The community observation protocol offers a set of guiding questions and focus areas for observing faculty and students working in the community as part of a service- or community-based learning course. The purposes of such observations are as follows:

- To describe the character and content of interactions between students/faculty and the community partner.

- To capture the dynamics of the community service experience, that is, the roles of students, faculty, and community partners.

- To document student learning in the community.

- To gather data on services rendered to the community (number of students, hours spent, kinds of services, clients served, etc.).

- To provide descriptive documentation of the partnership.

### Preparation

In preparation for observing in community settings, the following sequence is recommended:

1. Train and orient observers with practice observations in pairs to establish reliability.

2. Schedule time for introduction of assessment to students and community partners, introduction of observers and their roles, and completion of human subjects review protocols.

3. Involve faculty in determining which community settings and which days and times are most appropriate for observation. Observations should be planned with the faculty and the community partner.

### Administration

Observations should be conducted infrequently (once or twice during an academic quarter/semester) and be well coordinated with both the faculty and the community partner. Using the community observation protocol the observer will collect information about the following:

- Setting

- Roles of students, faculty, and community partners

- Interactions, communication, and activities taking place during community service

- Concerns expressed by students, faculty, and community partners

- Accomplishments, tasks, or service activities

- The climate (mood, affect)

The community observation protocol provides questions to be answered by the observer and focus areas for the observer to notice. It does not provide a format for recording observations. The intent is for observers to record narrative data in a journal or notebook. The narrative data should include direct quotations, specific examples, and (as much as possible) a record of what happens during the observation period. During actual recordings, the observer should maintain a neutral stance and try to avoid interpretation and critique. After writing a description of what was observed, the observer may write a summary of the observation. In the summary, it is appropriate to offer interpretation, raise questions, relate the observation to other information, and link observations to key study concepts.

## Analysis

Community observations contain rich data. Analysis of observational data is a complex process that requires a series of readings. The first reading is done to gain an overview of the data. The second reading is intended to surface themes or patterns in the data. The third and fourth readings are intended to confirm the themes or patterns, identify additional ones, and to begin to organize the data within the themes or patterns. The protocol questions and foci will emerge from the observational data as themes or patterns along with additional unanticipated ones. A format similar to that for reviewing and coding focus groups or interviews (see previous sections) can be used.

## Community Observation Protocol

1. Describe the setting: date of observation, location, arrangement of space, environment, mood, pace, and other factors.

2. Describe who is present and their apparent roles.

3. What actions are students taking (observer, leader, participant)? What actions are faculty taking? What actions are the community partners taking?

4. Describe the communications/interactions, and indicate the categories of individuals involved (e.g., students, partners, clients, etc.).

5. How does the community activity end? What sort of summation occurs ("next time, we will do some …" "good-bye," or nothing)?

6. What accomplishment(s), task(s), or service did you observe?

7. Were concerns expressed by students? By faculty? By community partner? What were they (provide descriptions of situations)?

8. Please add any other relevant observations.

# Community Focus Group

## Purpose
The purpose of a focus group with community partners is to use a facilitated group discussion to learn more about the experience of the partnership from the perspective of the community and to encourage reflection on ways to improve partnerships. Focus groups may also introduce community partners to each other and contribute to building social networks. A focus group usually lasts between one and one and a half hours, and provides rich and specific information for analysis of research themes.

## Preparation
In preparation for conducting a focus group, the following sequence is recommended:

- Identify a trained focus group facilitator and at least one observer/note-taker. This note-taker is responsible for ensuring equipment works throughout the focus group and for taking notes of non-verbal communication.

- Recruit 5-8 community partners to attend a focus group, working through faculty teaching service-learning classes.

- Establish a time and place convenient for the partners.

- The setting must offer a quiet room suitable for a circular seating layout.

- Ensure the availability of a good quality tape recorder.

- Arrange for parking for partners, and provide maps of the campus.

- Send a letter of instruction to partners and stress on-time arrival.

## Administration
It is essential that the facilitator be trained in focus group methods. Try to have the person arranging the focus group present at it, either as the note-taker or facilitator. This helps provide a personal connection for the partners. Logistical matters such as the following can contribute to a successful focus group:

- provide name tags for the partners (unless anonymity is critical)

- arrange participants in a circle or semi-circle

- facilitator opens session, describes purpose and gives ground rules using established script

- the role of the note-taker should be described, emphasizing that they are there to provide a back-up record should the tape recording not be audible

- participants should introduce themselves

- the introductory message on the following page should be read to the community partners prior to beginning the focus group questions

## Analysis

Tapes and notes from focus groups must be transcribed as soon as possible after the session. Focus groups generate a large body of rich, textual data. Analysis consists of organizing the data into meaningful subsections, initially according to the questions posed. Interpretation involves coding the data (identifying meaningful phrases and quotes) and searching for patterns within and across subsections. For a detailed discussion of analysis of focus group data, see Morgan (1993, 1997, 1998).

# Community Focus Group Protocol

## Introduction

The purposes of the focus group are twofold: to understand the impact of the partnership on the community-based organization, and to collect feedback, positive and negative, that will assist the university in improving partnership activities in the future. The discussion is recorded for the purpose of capturing detail, but all comments are confidential and never attributed to individual participants. As participants you can make the focus group successful by being both candid and as specific as possible when discussing different issues. A candid focus group will help the university document the effects of its efforts, recognize strengths and weaknesses of its outreach efforts, and identify areas where it can improve. As facilitator, I will offer no opinions; my role is to guide you through a conversation based on a set of relevant questions. I will try to make sure that everyone participates and that no one dominates the discussion. Please be sure to speak one at a time so the tape will be clear. During this discussion, please be brief and specific. Where there is disagreement, you should talk about your different perspective, but we will not spend time pressing for consensus or reaching agreement. The purpose is not to reach a common view, but to learn about all the possible views.

## Questions

1. Please introduce yourself and briefly describe the nature of your partnership with the university. (10 minutes)

2. What went well? What factors contributed to successful outcomes? What was the most important factor in achieving success? (10 minutes)

3. How would you describe the benefits of the partnership from your perspective? Any economic benefits? What was the value of the outcome? Any new insights into operations? Was there any impact on capacity to serve clients? (10 minutes)

4. How would you describe the burdens (if any) of the partnership? [Probe: Demands on time or staff.] (10 minutes)

5. What obstacles or barriers affected the partnership? [Probe: How did you cope with these?] (5 minutes)

6. What would you do differently next time? What one thing would you change? (5 minutes)

7. What might the university do differently next time? What would you change about the university if you could? (10 minutes)

8. What do you know about the university that you didn't know before? What do you wish you knew more about? (10 minutes)

9. How would you describe this experience to a colleague in another community organization or agency? What would you emphasize? (10 minutes)

10. The final thing we will do is to encourage you to reflect again on your experience of working with the university. Reflect back over the project period and over this discussion. What's the most important thing you'd like the university to hear from you? What have we not discussed? (10 minutes)

11. Are there any other comments you would like to share?

Total time: 1 hour, 30 minutes

Thank participants.

## Community Partner Interview

### Purpose

Community partner interviews are intended to foster a one-on-one conversation with a community partner to explore their perspectives on the experience of working with the university. This instrument could be used to assess a wide variety of community-university interactions.

### Preparation

Schedule one-hour interviews in locations and at times convenient to the community partner. In advance, describe the purpose of the interview so the partner may reflect on issues of impact prior to the interview session.

### Administration

The administration of interviews should be consistent across all interview subjects. Following are some guidelines:

- start on time

- introduce yourself and your role in the project

- explain the purpose of the interview

- assure confidentiality

- stress the importance of candor

- take notes or ask permission to tape record

- follow protocol carefully and keep probes neutral

### Analysis

Transcribe notes and/or tapes immediately. Code transcripts for key words and themes. Organize these into patterns and compare to research variables.

## Community Interview Partner Protocol

Let's begin with some basic information:

1.  Please provide a brief overview, from your own perspective, of the partnership project in which your organization participated.

2.  Why did you get involved in this partnership? How did it come about?

Let's talk about the outcomes of the project:

3.  What were your expectations? Did you have specific goals? Were your expectations met?

4.  What would you say was the key to success? What went particularly well, and why?

5.  What obstacles/barriers did you encounter and how did you deal with them?

We're interested in the impact of the project on your organization:

6.  What were the benefits to your organization (social, economic, impacts on staff, insights about operations, capacity to serve clients)?

7.  Knowing what you know now, what would you do differently that would make the partnership go better?

Thinking about the university's role in the partnership:

8.  What should the university do differently next time?

The final thing we will do is to encourage you to reflect again on your experience of working with the university. Reflect back over the project period and over this discussion:

9.  What is the most important thing you'd like the university to hear from you?

10. What relationship, if any, do you anticipate you will develop/maintain with the university in the future?


Thank participant.

## Community Survey

### Purpose

The community survey is intended to describe community partners' perspectives, motivations, concerns, and attitudes on issues related to their experience with students through a service-learning course. The survey is based on a five point Likert scale where partners report their level of agreement regarding their experience with students and faculty. The scale range includes "strongly disagree," "disagree," "neutral," "agree," and "strongly agree." Topics assessed by the survey include community partner's observations about their interactions with the university, the challenges they encountered, the effects of the interactions, their influence on the university, and their overall satisfaction with their connection to the university. The community survey was developed through a process of literature review, survey of existing instruments, and discussions with community partners and faculty.

The information gained through the community partner survey is useful for purposes of planning programs to orient community partners, faculty, and students to working together on service-learning or community-based learning courses.

### Preparation

Before administering the community partner survey the following preparation steps are recommended.

1. Determine the purpose of instrument use. The decisions include determining if the instrument is to be used in a pre-post assessment of change or in a post-test only approach to describe the general attitudes and perceptions of community partners after they have participated in a service-learning course.

2. Consider using other data-gathering strategies to complement use of the community partner survey to develop a more complete and useful profile of partner perspectives. This instrument is ideally used prior to conducting community partner interviews or focus groups. To gain a full picture of a course, the community partner survey will complement data yielded by the student and faculty surveys.

3. Determine appropriate scheduling of the instrument use. Usually the best time is soon after the course has ended.

4. Solicit partner consent and support for the instrument use. Well in advance of sending out the community partner survey, partners should be informed of its purpose and their consent established, preferably in writing.

### Administration

Once the preparation steps are complete, the following administration procedures are recommended for use of the community partner survey.

1. Partner anonymity should be assured and maintained throughout the collection of data from the survey.

2. Partners should be informed that the instrument will take 15-20 minutes to complete.

3. Clear information should be included about returning the survey (timing and where to return the form).

## Analysis

Data analysis can be conducted through utilization of the Statistical Package for Social Sciences (SPSS) software. In the case of assessing and comparing pre- and post-service-learning experiences, the analysis could include frequencies, descriptive statistics, Chi-squares, Analyses of Variance (ANOVA), and factor analysis. First, descriptive statistics and frequencies serve as a database, providing mean, mode, and standard deviation between items. Second, Chi-squares correlate descriptive data among partners. Third, Factor Analysis reduces items into categories that are closely related. Finally, ANOVA's are useful to explore the existence of variation among partners on either single items or groups of items that may arise from the factor analysis.

## Community-Based Learning — Community Partner Survey

We would like to better understand the impact that community-based learning has on our community partners. Please assist us by taking 5-10 minutes to complete this survey, and return it to [directions personalized to institution].

### I. First we would like some information about you.

1. How long have you been working with our university?
   - ❑ Less than one year   ❑ 1-3 years   ❑ More than 3 years

2. What is your organizational status?
   - ❑ Public        OR        ❑ Private
   - ❑ For-profit    OR        ❑ Nonprofit

3. What are the benchmark areas addressed by your organization? (check all appropriate)
   - ❑ Education    ❑ Housing      ❑ Safety
   - ❑ Health       ❑ Environment  ❑ Public Services

### II. The next set of questions relates to your most recent experiences with our university.

4. How did your interactions with the university influence your capacity to fulfil the mission of your organization? *Mark any that apply.*
   - ❑ New insights about the organization/its operation
   - ❑ Increase in number of clients served
   - ❑ Enhanced offerings of services
   - ❑ Increased leverage of financial/other resources
   - ❑ New connections/networks with other community groups
   - ❑ Changes in organizational direction
   - ❑ Increases in number of services offered
   - ❑ No influence
   - ❑ Other influences (specify) _____

5. What are some of the challenges you encountered? *Mark any that apply.*
   - ❑ Demands upon staff time
   - ❑ Project time period insufficient
   - ❑ Students not well prepared
   - ❑ Number of students inappropriate for size of organization
   - ❑ Mismatch between course goals and organization
   - ❑ Little contact/interaction with faculty
   - ❑ Students did not perform as expected
   - ❑ Other (please specify) _____

6. What were some of the economic effects of your work with the university? *Mark any that apply.*
   - ❑ Increased value of services
   - ❑ Increased organizational resources
   - ❑ Completion of projects
   - ❑ Access to university technology and expertise
   - ❑ New products, services, materials generated
   - ❑ Increased funding opportunities
   - ❑ Identification of new staff
   - ❑ Identification of additional volunteers
   - ❑ Other (please specify) _____

7. In what ways do you believe that you are able to influence the university as a result of your connection with one of our courses? *Mark any that apply.*
   - ❑ Influence on course content
   - ❑ Influence on university policies
   - ❑ Influence on faculty awareness of community
   - ❑ Influence on student learning experience
   - ❑ Other (please specify) _____

8. As a result of your connection to this university course, how has your awareness of the university changed? *Mark any that apply.*
   ❏ I learned more about university programs & services
   ❏ I know whom to call upon for information and assistance
   ❏ I am more involved with activities on campus
   ❏ I have an increased knowledge of university resources
   ❏ I have more interactions with faculty and administrators
   ❏ I have taken or plan to take classes at the university
   ❏ Other (please specify) _____

9. Do you plan to continue working with the university in this or another activity?
   ❏ Yes        ❏ No

**III. Please rate your level of satisfaction with your connection to a university course in the following areas.**

| | Strongly Agree | Agree | Neutral | Disagree | Strongly Disagree |
|---|---|---|---|---|---|
| 10. Overall communication with students and faculty. | ❏ | ❏ | ❏ | ❏ | ❏ |
| 11. Level and quality of interaction with students/faculty. | ❏ | ❏ | ❏ | ❏ | ❏ |
| 12. Quality of student work. | ❏ | ❏ | ❏ | ❏ | ❏ |
| 13. Feedback and input into planning of experiences. | ❏ | ❏ | ❏ | ❏ | ❏ |
| 14. Scope and timing of activity. | ❏ | ❏ | ❏ | ❏ | ❏ |
| 15. Level of trust with faculty and students. | ❏ | ❏ | ❏ | ❏ | ❏ |

16. How did you handle the logistics of your community-based learning course? *Please mark the one most accurate response.*
   ❏ I made the arrangements and placements.
   ❏ The faculty member made the arrangements and placements.
   ❏ A graduate student made the arrangements and placements.
   ❏ We handled the arrangements and placements collaboratively.
   ❏ Students handled their own placements.

17. What was the best aspect of this experience for you?

18. What aspects of the experience would you change?

19. Please add any other additional comments.

*Thank you for your comments.*
*Please return this by [insert date] to [insert relevant mailing address].*

# Institutional Impact

## Why Assess Institutional Factors?

As more and more institutions create service-learning opportunities for their students, the intensive influence of organizational context becomes clearer. From the earliest stages of campus discussion about the potential role of service-learning, institutional factors affect decision-making at every level and every stage of operations. In addition, some institutional explorations of service-learning begin with executive leadership (top-down) and some begin with faculty initiative (bottom-up). In those cases, a campus may struggle to foster communication and agreement across the organization on the level of commitment to service-learning. Assessment can be a tool for addressing internal obstacles to service-learning, fostering communications and shared understanding, and identifying areas where institutional change is needed.

Service-learning programs are always strongly influenced by their institutional environments. The impact of organizational context on service-learning and engagement endeavors means that systematic assessment of institutional factors can play an extremely important role in facilitating campus commitment by providing relevant and neutral data to inform decision-making and reduce obstacles.

Consider the potential uses of institutional assessment findings by different institutional sectors. Assessment is useful to senior administrators seeking to expand faculty interest and involvement by providing evidence that service-learning enhances student learning, leverages financial resources, enhances institutional reputation and community relations, and improves faculty satisfaction with their careers. Assessment of the institutional context can also be useful to faculty governance leaders or departmental chairs by providing evidence that service-learning is worth doing, assisting in documenting activities for consideration in promotion and tenure decisions, and convincing administrative leaders to support and invest in service-learning programs. Individual faculty can use assessment to show an impact beyond their individual service-learning course, or to make the case with other faculty or administrators for the value of service-learning.

Assessment of institutional factors also helps ensure quality and consistency in the organization's design of service-learning experiences so as to ensure that the institution's overall relationship with the external community is enhanced. Even when service-learning courses are self-initiated by individual faculty, the institutional context will have an impact on the experience and on community perception. For example, every faculty member and every student carries the aura of the institution with them when they encounter members of the external community and engage in an exchange of knowledge such as occurs in service-learning activities. This is particularly true for those institutions with a strong public commitment to service-learning and civic engagement. The image and public perceptions of the institution will be translated into the seemingly more individual and personal encounter between campus and community that is inherent in service-learning. In addition, every faculty member, student, and course must exist within an academic and institutional culture that, while espousing academic freedom and autonomy, also creates value and belief structures that define what is possible and what is likely to receive support. Assessment findings can help highlight these internal and external relationship and culture issues, and identify areas where improvement is needed.

When we began to create this model for assessing service-learning, we realized that many of the impacts on students, faculty, and community were strongly influenced by institutional factors that also warranted assessment. The emphasis on gathering information that promotes program improvement compelled us to include the study of institutional factors. Simply stated, most of the factors addressed in the assessment of impact on faculty, students, and community are linked to institutional and organizational issues. Any improvements in service-learning will be difficult without an understanding of institutional issues. In other words, assessment of institutional factors cuts across and complements all of the other constituent assessments.

## Understanding Institutional Commitment to Service-Learning

Before designing an institutional assessment, there must be a clear articulation of institutional goals for, and interests in, service-learning. Service-learning programs are complex and do not develop in isolation from institutional contexts. An important resource that can guide an initial discussion of campus interest in service-learning is the President's Declaration on the Civic Responsibility of Higher Education (Campus Compact, 1998). This report was developed by a group of higher education presidents discussing their commitment to civic education, and views service-learning as one of the relevant teaching and learning methods. The declaration begins with a useful discussion of the need for every institution to consider its civic mission. Of particular value to a campus seeking to develop an institutional assessment, the Declaration includes a discussion guide for assessing campus activities and structures related to civic responsibility. This could guide the development of agreement on the vision and goals for service-learning programs. These goals become the foundation of an assessment plan that measures institutional impact.

A review of recent and relevant literature highlights how central the role of institutional context is to the scope, scale, and styles of service-learning. It also demonstrates why assessment of institutional impact and factors is essential to assessment for improvement of service-learning endeavors (Bringle & Hatcher, 2000; Bucco & Busch, 1996; Holland, 1997; Rubin, 1996; Ward, 1996). The design, implementation, and sustainability of service-learning programs is most often shaped by institutional interpretations of the following broad factors:

- campus mission

- academic culture/traditions

- political/governance environment

- financial condition

- institutional history, self-image, sense of peers

- public image/reputation

- student traits/goals

- community conditions/needs/assets

Some commonalities emerge when looking at more detailed aspects of academic organizations among the same authors. The following organizational factors, most commonly mentioned, also have a dramatic influence on the shape and impact of service-learning programs:

- infrastructure for service

- faculty development investments

- community involvement

- campus policy and reward systems

- commitment to evaluation

- curricular and co-curricular service activities (links exist between academic and student affairs)

- existing, relevant initiatives

- resource allocation choices

- leadership across institutional levels

- support for interdisciplinary work

- communications strategies/dissemination

As any institution begins creating service-learning opportunities, or initiates an assessment of the outcomes of existing service-learning courses and programs, the discussion is influenced by the campus interpretation, values, and beliefs around these factors. How they shape the service-learning programs depends on campus goals and objectives for service-learning. We see this happening when one looks across institutions that seem outwardly similar in mission and capacity, but some adopt service-learning more readily than others. Why does this happen? Each campus's exploration of the impact of the factors listed above reveals deeper underlying differences among institutions; these differences make service-learning more appropriate and readily accepted at some institutions than at others.

Part of a campus's interpretation of these major factors is a consideration of institutional motivation. Why service-learning? What is our reason for taking on this work? What are our goals and hopes? Institutional motivations can be summarized in three dimensions:

- self-interest

- good citizenship/good works

- enhanced academic performance (new directions in research and learning for faculty and students) that realizes a distinct sense of campus mission

Most institutions develop some balance across these three dimensions. For example, everything we do in academia should have some element of self-interest. We do not have the resources to be wasteful of time and effort. However, if we act purely out of self-interest, as when a campus may buy up several blocks of real estate near campus to "clean up" an area the campus perceives as blighted and call it a "service to the community," then there is an imbalance with the other dimensions that are vital to successful campus-community partnerships. Focusing purely on good works can also have some detriments as it tends to leave the community in the role of supplicant and may give students a mixed message about issues of privilege, class, and social responsibility.

For most institutions, the adoption of service-learning strategies is meant to enhance academics by more clearly articulating the distinctive learning and working environment the campus offers to its faculty and students, in keeping with its sense of mission. This choice of strategies can reflect elements of self-interest (hoped for improvements in student recruitment, faculty satisfaction, fund-raising opportunities, and/or public image and community relations, to name a few). Commitment to service-learning also requires the institution to define its goals for itself as a good citizen of the region. How will community partnerships, such as those created for service-learning courses, connect the academic assets of the campus to the issues, needs and opportunities of the community or region? In this way, we can understand and explain differences in levels of institutional commitment to service-learning, or to other forms of civic engagement and campus-community partnerships.

A framework that can be used to guide an institution's self-examination of its mission is shown in Table 8 (Holland, 1997). This table directs attention toward seven key organizational factors often associated with commitment to service, and then describes the features that indicate different levels of commitment to service or service-learning. There is no judgment of goodness or success/failure across the four descriptive levels; they merely illustrate in measurable terms the differences that can occur across institutions regarding levels of commitment. The intent is that institutions can candidly interpret their vision and goals for service-learning, and then explore the alignment of organizational characteristics with that vision. In other words, each individual campus can seek to align the rhetoric and the reality of its commitment to service. The process also identifies areas where change must occur to promote alignment of commitment with program goals.

Each of the seven factors is critical to the implementation and sustainability of service endeavors, such as service-learning. Understanding the institution's goals and ambitions for adopting service-learning strategies allows a campus community, or a single department or school, to design programs with an understanding of the impact of the institutional context on the operation of those programs.

With that understanding, a plan for regular assessment of these institutional factors, and others, can be used to document the impact of service-learning on the institution (including both unintended and intended impacts). This documentation can then be used to make improvements that will enhance and sustain the service-learning effort and the underlying community partnership.

## The Assessment Matrix for Institutional Factors

Earlier in this work, we described the basic process for translating service-learning goals into variables or concepts from which measurable indicators could be developed. Table 9 offers an example of key concepts, indicators, and methods for measurement relevant to the assessment of the dynamic relationship between service-learning and the institutional context.

Given the discussion above on key organizational factors that are known to be essential in setting goals and expectations for service-learning within the context of a campus' mission and conditions, the selection of concepts and indicators should consider at least two broad purposes of the institutional assessment. Local circumstances or special issue projects may add additional purposes.

First, the concepts and indicators should be a tool for tracking progress toward aligning the institutional environment with the service-learning effort. In other words, the assessment effort should focus, at least in part, on areas where the organization needs to make changes to support service-learning. By looking for impact (or the absence of impact), measures should also help to identify new or additional changes/improvements in the institutional environment that may be needed as work goes forward.

Second, the concepts and indicators should be designed with the intent of capturing changes in actions and relationships among students, faculty, community, and institution, according to the goals of the service-learning program.

**Engagement in community** assesses the overall institutional involvement in the community. Service-learning often benefits from an organizational context in which other kinds of partnership relationships exist between campus and community. The concept looks for that context of the exchange relationship.

**Orientation to teaching and learning** relates back to Table 1 in the chapter on Assessment Principles and Strategies in this monograph. Because the Portland State University service-learning program sought to change the teaching/learning environment for faculty and students this was an important factor to track. It is measured by looking at both quantitative and qualitative levels of activity meant to influence faculty attitudes toward their teaching strategies and the role of service in their scholarly agenda.

**Resource acquisition** can be a strong test of institutional commitment and progress in that it examines the links between activities and revenue streams. Obvious and useful measures include looking at the degree to which issues of service-learning and community engagement are reflected in grant-making and fund-raising strategies. In another setting, it might also be important to look at the re-allocation of existing resources as a measure of commitment.

**Image/reputation** recognizes that the campus has some degree of self-interest in expanding service-learning or other engagement endeavors. Faculty motivation and donor/gift support can be strongly influenced by evidence that service-learning is shaping the image and reputation of the institution in the eyes of the community and decision-makers. In addition, the presence of service-related issues in campus searches and reports such as those for accreditation can be revealing of the level of acceptance and centrality.

**The visibility** the campus gives to service in its own communications and publications is a good measure of the depth and breadth of commitment. We found measures of recognition and celebration through written word or leadership action to be a revealing reflection of the support for service-learning.

One of the most central factors related to the effectiveness and sustainability of service-learning is the presence of necessary **supportive infrastructure**. This recognizes the labor-intensive and time-consuming nature of service activities and measures institutional investment in services and policies that are essential to sustaining and promoting service-learning courses and the partnerships that support them.

**Leadership at all levels** of the organization is also essential to the sustainability and/or expansion of service-learning programs. We propose several potential measures that look at the nature of internal attention to decisions that support service, and to external activities and relationships that signal the level of commitment and interest among campus leaders.

Thus, we see that institutional factors cut across student, faculty, and community partner issues and relationships. The key concepts proposed in Table 9 are fairly broad, but the indicators include specific measures intended to document changes or effects on the three constituent groups involved in service-learning. For example, some measures track contacts between community and the institution, changes in student involvement in the community, changes in faculty priorities, or visibility of service endeavors in campus messages. Each constituent group involved in a service-learning program affects the institution by their actions, and in turn is affected by the institution's actions and policies. This provides the rationale for multiple measures for each factor, and a multi-dimensional approach to data collection.

## Strategies for Assessing Institutional Impact

In Table 9, methods for collecting data to measure the indicators are offered. The potential sources for institutional data can be numerous in an environment where institutional data is openly shared. As may be the case in student and faculty dimensions of assessment, access to some data can be an assessment challenge. A critical factor can be the level of institutional attention to data collection. Some smaller institutions may not have the resources to conduct unique or regular studies that would create data relevant to a service-learning assessment. Interest in assessment can lead to creating new strategies and capacities for collecting data efficiently. For example, an office working with service-learning students may be willing to keep a simple log on questions from students or the community.

Whatever methods are used, attention to terminology and definitions is essential to ensure that relevant data is gathered. We encourage individuals to engage the constituent groups in instrument design and testing so as to generate some common understanding of terms such as service-learning, service, outcomes, and engagement. Many surveys of faculty seeking to learn about their service activities, for example, have low return rates because faculty are not clear on the meaning of some of the terms.

Though diverse methods are suggested in the matrix, the strategy for collecting assessment data on institutions is basically two-fold: talk to a wide variety of people, and tap into information and documents that already exist. Creativity and persistence are essential qualities of the investigator assessing institutional factors. The search is for evidence that campus commitment to service is being recognized, supported, and acknowledged in a number of ways. Is the level of support and awareness increasing or decreasing over time? Here is just a short sample of potential resources that can help generate data relevant to the indicators in our assessment plan:

- **Publications such as newsletters, alumni magazines, posters:** Do they mention service-learning programs or outcomes?

- **Annual reports:** Do they highlight service-learning as part of the mission? Is the institution attracting gifts or grants relevant to service-learning efforts? Is it a fundraising priority?

- **Student application essays:** Why are they coming to your campus? Is it because of the commitment to service?

- **Activity logs:** Are more or fewer community calls coming into key offices on campus? What is the purpose of the calls?

- **Media reports:** Is the media talking about your service-learning partnerships?

- **Catalog/course schedules:** Do these highlight or identify service-learning courses in any way?

- **Existing surveys:** Will your institutional research office add questions to standing surveys of students, faculty or alumni?

- **Budget narratives/requests/allocations:** Is service-learning part of your institution's budget design? What is the investment in support infrastructure over time?

- **Interviews:** What do your admissions counselors tell inquiring applicants about service-learning opportunities and about the institution's commitment to service?

- **Policies:** Is there/has there been any change in faculty portfolios for promotion, merit or tenure? Are they including information about service-learning? What are the outcomes of the reviews? Are there policies supporting faculty development related to service? Are there incentives for faculty to adopt service-learning in their courses? Are there awards of recognition for faculty and students engaged in service, as there are for good teaching and academic performance?

## Concluding Thoughts

In some ways assessment of institutional impact and factors may be the most important element of assessment of service-learning. Because institutional contexts have such a strong influence on the perceptions and actions of faculty, students, and community, understanding and monitoring the institutional environment is critical to moving all other aspects of service-learning forward.

Institutions that are making advanced commitments to service-learning have made the investment in assessing their level of commitment to civic engagement, explored the alignment of that commitment to organizational structure and policies, and identified and addressed need for organizational changes. Other institutions begin service-learning only to discover competing internal and external views of the campus mission, priorities, motives, and relationships to the community. In such an environment, service-learning and other engagement activities can become marginalized and necessary organizational changes may encounter substantial resistance.

Assessment of institutional environment may be one remedy to this situation. The institution's cross-cutting affect on all other dimensions of service-learning makes the investment in interpreting institutional impact essential. The loosely-coupled nature of academic organizations and the evidentiary orientation of academic culture means that change and innovation in higher education is largely dependent on the ability of institutional leaders and provocateurs to generate evidence through research and assessment. A major challenge in implementing necessary assessment strategies is the historic under-investment in institutional research and assessment capacities. An interesting, unintended effect arising from the growing implementation of civic engagement and service-learning programs is a greater level of institutional awareness of the need for assessment infrastructure. Thus, we may find that measuring the institution's capacity to conduct assessment may be a critical factor to be monitored in an assessment plan.

**Table 8: Levels of Commitment to Service, Characterized by Key Organizational Factors Evidencing Relevance to Institutional Mission**

| | Level One Low Relevance | Level Two Medium Relevance | Level Three High Relevance | Level Four Full Integration |
|---|---|---|---|---|
| **Mission** | No mention or undefined rhetorical reference | Service is part of what we do as citizens | Service is an element of our academic agenda | Service is a central and defining characteristic |
| **Promotion, Tenure, Hiring** | Service to campus committees or to discipline | Community service mentioned; volunteerism or consulting may be included in portfolio | Formal guidelines for defining, documenting and rewarding service | Community-based research and teaching are key criteria for hiring and evaluation |
| **Organization Structure** | None focused on service or volunteerism | Units may exist to foster volunteerism | Various separate centers and institutes are organized to provide service | Infrastructure exists to support widespread faculty and student participation |
| **Student Involvement & Curriculum** | Part of extracurricular student life activities | Organized support for volunteer activity | Opportunity for extra credit, internships, practicum experience, special events/activities | Service learning and community-based learning featured across curriculum |
| **Faculty Involvement** | Service defined only as campus duties; committees; little interdisciplinary work | Pro bono consulting; community volunteerism acknowledged | Tenured/senior faculty pursue community-based research; some teach service-learning courses | Community research and active learning a high priority; interdisciplinary and collaborative work is encouraged |
| **Community Involvement** | Random or limited individual or group involvement | Community representation on advisory boards for departments or schools | Community influences campus through active partnerships or part-time teaching or participation in service learning programs | Community involved in defining, conducting and evaluating community-based research and teaching |
| **Campus Publications** | Community engagement not an emphasis | Stories of student volunteerism or alumni as good citizens | Emphasis on economic impact, role of campus centers/institutes | Community connection as key to mission; fundraising has engagement as a focus |

Barbara A. Holland, 2001. Adapted from "Analyzing Institutional Commitment to Service," *Michigan Journal of Community Service Learning*, Vol. 4, Fall 1997, pp. 30–41.

## Table 9: Matrix for Institutional Assessment

| What do we want to know? (concepts) | How will we know it? (indicators) | How will we measure it? (methods) | Who/what will provide the data? (sources) |
|---|---|---|---|
| Engagement in community | Requests for assistance from community<br>Number of service-learning courses, community–university partnerships<br>Level of student club activity in community service<br>Level of community use of campus facilities<br>Attendance at partnership events | Activity logs<br>Schedule/catalog analysis<br>Grants analysis/reports<br>Facility/budget records<br>Interviews | Institutional sources<br>Faculty<br>Administrators<br>Community partners |
| Orientation to teaching and learning | Number and variety of faculty adopting service-learning<br>Total number of service-learning courses offered/approved<br>Focus/content of faculty development programming<br>Departmental agendas/budgets for service<br>Number of faculty publications related to service | Survey of faculty activity<br>Schedule/catalog analysis<br>Interviews of chairs<br>Budget report analysis<br>CV analysis | Institutional sources<br>Faculty<br>Administrators |
| Resource acquisition | Number of grant proposals/funded projects with community components<br>Inclusion of service-related requests in development and fund-raising<br>Level of giving to service-related donor funds<br>Recognition/grants from foundations/others related to service-learning | Grants analysis<br>Publications analysis<br>Gift records<br>Activity logs | Institutional sources<br>Faculty<br>Administrators |
| Image/reputation | Media coverage: campus, local, regional, national<br>Site visits by other campus teams or expertCommunity partners<br>Representation at conferences and in publications<br>Quality and diversity of new faculty/administrator applicants<br>Content of accreditation self-studies and reviews by site teams | Clipping/Video reports<br>Activity logs<br>Personnel records<br>Publication analysis<br>Interviews | Institutional sources<br>Faculty<br>Administrators<br>Community partners |
| Visibility of service and service-learning on campus | Content of campus publications, schedules, videos, web pages<br>Awards of recognition for faculty, students, staff, partners<br>Volunteer service by staff, administration, faculty, students<br>Celebratory events related to service or including community | Interviews<br>Survey<br>Publication analysis<br>Observation | Institutional records<br>Faculty/staff<br>Community partners<br>Students |
| Infrastructure | Presence of organized support for service<br>Dollars invested in infrastructure, faculty incentives, faculty development<br>Policy context: content of faculty handbook, student handbook | Organization charts<br>Budget reports/requests<br>Document analysis | Institutional sources |
| Leadership | Local, regional, national roles of campus leaders<br>Content of budget narratives, speeches or self-studies<br>Community event participation<br>Characteristics/qualifications of new hires | Document analysis<br>Clipping/videos<br>Interviews<br>CV analysis | Institutional sources<br>Faculty<br>Administrators |

# Strategies and Methods: Institution

## Institutional Interviews

### Purpose

Interviews help to explore the perspectives of university staff and administrators on the role of community-based education activities, particularly of the impact of community partnerships on the university's operations and goals. This method can also be used to discern the level of campus understanding regarding community-university partnerships and the ability to articulate the university's community activities.

### Preparation

Representatives from institutional administration should be identified based on their ability to provide insights about the work being assessed. New faculty might be interviewed in order to better understand their perceptions of the institution, as well as to assess the impact of targeted recruitment strategies.

Schedule one-hour interviews in locations and at convenient times for the interviewee. In advance, describe the purpose of the interview so the subject has time to reflect on issues of impact prior to the interview session.

### Administration

The administration of interviews should be consistent across all interview subjects:

- start on time

- introduce yourself and your role in the project

- explain purposes of interview

- assure confidentiality; stress importance of candor

- take notes or ask permission to tape record

The following offices are possible sources for interviews. Their representatives can be interviewed for perspectives on the role and impact of community-based education on the institution:

- Academic Affairs

- Alumni Office

- Admissions Office

- Advising Offices

- Faculty Development Centers

- Foundation Office

- Grants and Contracts Office

- Health Services

- Institutional Research Office

- Student Services (Other)

- Teaching and Learning Center

- Undergraduate Studies Administrators (e.g., general education office)

**Analysis**

Transcribe notes and/or tapes immediately. Code transcripts for key words and themes. Organize these into patterns and compare to research variables.

## Institutional Interview Protocol: Representatives from University Offices

*[Narrative introduction to set context.]*

1. What is your understanding of the university mission and academic environment? How do you describe it to others (prospective students/staff/faculty)?

2. Are you involved in any community-university interactions? Describe what and why.

3. Is community service part of your professional or personal life? Describe your activities and reasons for involvement.

4. What are the distinguishing characteristics of the "student experience" at the university?

5. Are you aware of university courses that include a component of service- or community-based learning? If yes, what do you know about them and how did you learn of them?

6. Do you tell prospective students/staff/faculty that the university offers service-learning courses or engages in community partnerships? Why or why not?

7. What effect do you think community-university partnerships have on the university's institutional image and how do you know?

8. Should the campus offer more service-learning courses and make service-learning a core of the student learning experience?

9. Is there anything else you would like to tell me today?

Thank interviewee.

## Institutional Interview Protocol: New Faculty

*[Provide introduction to set context.]*

1. In your hiring process were the university's community partnerships described to you? How were they described?

2. Have you heard about the university's service- or community-based learning courses? How were they described? Are you interested in teaching such courses?

3. Have you seen the promotion and tenure guidelines for this university?

4. What attracted you to this university (or use institution name)?

5. What are the goals for your work at this institution (or use name)?

6. Is there anything else you would like to tell me today about this topic?

Thank interviewee.

## Critical Incident Report

### Purpose

Completion of a critical incident report provides an opportunity to identify key highlights and issues that have occurred during a program or designated period of time. The report is highly reflective, and offers a retrospective review of major events (anticipated or unanticipated) that affected the program in positive or negative ways.

Critical incident reports complement other methods of data collection, and can provide an overview of how program development issues affect outcomes. They are also useful to document the processes involved in program administration from a broad perspective over time (rather than a daily log).

### Administration

Identify key individuals who are closely connected to the program and have the experience and insights to identify critical incidents. For example, if an institution is adopting a major strategy to implement service-learning, then the key university administrators responsible (such as a vice-provost, a director of a teaching and learning center, the academic program director of a service-learning program) would be invited to complete a critical incident report.

Directions for completing a critical incident report should be very specific, and should include documentation of key events that, in retrospect, significantly:

- accelerated work toward accomplishment of goals, and/or

- created barriers to goal accomplishment, and/or

- enabled the organization to overcome these barriers.

Examples of critical incidents might include adoption of relevant institutional policy on service-learning, grants awarded (or not awarded), key staff member(s) hired or terminated, physical relocation of offices, new faculty promotion and tenure criteria adopted, accreditation report received, etc.

### Preparation

The most useful format for presentation of a critical incident is to set up a table with three columns:

1. Date (specific or approximation via month alone), with events listed in chronological order

2. Nature of event

3. Why it is/was critical

An example is presented on the next page.

## Sample Critical Incident Report

| Date | Nature of event | Why critical |
|------|-----------------|--------------|
| June 2000 | New P&T criteria approved | These criteria explicitly acknowledge the value of the scholarship of outreach as part of the institution's commitment to civic engagement. They will help to encourage faculty to participate, as a clear linkage between service-learning and tenure/promotion is now our policy. |
| September 2000 | $180,000 grant from the Civic Foundation received | This grant will support faculty development programs, mini-grants to faculty wishing to develop service-learning courses, and travel funds to attend conferences. |
| October 2000 | Accreditation report received from regional accreditor | Report very critical of our lack of assessment data, with specific attention to our lack of documentation of the impact of our service-learning activities. Provost extremely unhappy, and mandated new assessment task force to act. |

## Analysis

It is usually most helpful to be able to collect critical incident reports from several individuals with their own perspectives on a program's progression. Their critical incident reports can then be merged into a single chronology to develop an overall perspective on the key informants' perspectives. If this is done, care needs to be taken to avoid identifying individuals — the point is not to gain consensus, but rather to get a full-view perspective on events. Where different opinions are offered on the same event, include each as a separate entry in the chronology.

Once the reports are integrated, develop a framework based on your indicators and key concepts in which you can record key findings from the critical incident reports (sometimes creating a table or a blank matrix is useful). This helps to guide thinking through the review of the various documents and will help maintain a focus on the key concepts and indicators.

The framework can then be reviewed to search for patterns in the findings, and these patterns can be compared to other findings from other methods. Write a brief narrative to reflect your findings, and integrate this narrative into your overall report. Remember that this method is intended to complement other findings; it should not be used as a stand-alone method of data collection.

## Institutional Observations

A component of institutionalization and sustainability involves the level of reciprocity and interaction between campus and community. Observation of campus events, public events, and campus or community advisory meetings can be revealing. Questions that might serve as the basis for designing observation include the following:

- Who attends public events on or off campus?

- Are community leaders invited to and present at campus events?

- Who serves on advisory boards, how often do they meet, and what are their duties?

- Do campus activities and space management offer opportunities for a community presence on campus?

- Is the institution included in or involved in major public community events?

- How is participation in major public community events supported?

Refer to the classroom observation (p. 66) or the community observation (p. 94) for more detail or approaches to observation, and then adapt these approaches in light of your own assessment goals and institutional contexts/dynamics.

## Institutional Documentation

### Sources

Many institutions have documentation available that can be analyzed to augment understanding of impact of community-based education. Examples of those artifacts and documents include the following:

- records of gift giving

- media coverage of the institution (newspaper articles, television spots, etc.)

- student awards

- attendance logs from faculty development events (workshops, seminars)

- internal newsletters describing faculty achievements, curriculum changes, etc.

- student retention data

- admissions data

- alumni survey data

- promotion and tenure guidelines

- course schedules and catalog

- program descriptions

- web pages

- recruitment publications

- annual reports

- strategic planning and budget documents

- president/provost speeches

- publications for donors/alumni

### Analysis

When analyzing artifacts and documents, decide ahead of time what indicators from your assessment matrix you will be looking for in these sources. In general you are looking for evidence that service-learning and other forms of community-campus partnerships and civic engagement activities are being highlighted in publications, and in internal and external communications. Stories of faculty, student, and community interactions suggest a level of centrality and commitment that are vital to sustainability. Text of program descriptions, course descriptions, and the content of catalogs and course schedules can also reveal the presence or absence of attention to the visibility and availability of service-learning courses.

A special note on the use of existing surveys: Institutional data reports or survey findings can also be useful sources for quantitative evidence of faculty, student, or alumni involvement in service.

Most institutions conduct a regular panel of surveys regarding current students, alumni, and others. A good strategy is to negotiate the inclusion of a few questions relevant to service-learning and engagement issues. This will lead to regularly-collected quantitative data which can be useful to measure longitudinal impact on individuals.

# Methods and Analysis

*I*n the preceding sections that offer examples of assessment instruments for faculty, students, institutions, and community, each instrument was preceded by brief suggestions and guidelines for administering and analyzing those instruments. From our field research we have learned that many people who have assessment responsibilities may have limited or dated knowledge of quantitative and qualitative research methods and analysis techniques. (Remember how you hated that graduate statistics class [if you took one ... ] and promptly erased it all from your mind?!) Assessment strategies that seem difficult to implement or sustain, or that produce findings that confuse or challenge those who must interpret the reports, can often be traced to poor use of instruments or poor analysis. Many assessment leaders take on these roles because of interest and passion, and they do not always have deep technical expertise or access to those with more skills.

Therefore, this section on methods and analysis offers deeper and more detailed guidance on the design, use, and analysis of various instruments commonly used in assessment programs, particularly in higher education.[1] For each major type of method, we offer points about definition, common uses, questions, structures, and formats, and follow these with suggestions for administration and analysis. Obviously, even this lengthier section does not cover all there is to know about these methods; whole textbooks have been written on each one. The authors hope these more detailed guidelines will serve most purposes for assessment leaders, and we refer readers to the bibliography for further guidance and study on methods and analysis.

---

[1]The following section was originally published in: Sherril B. Gelmon and Amy Connell. (2000). *Program Evaluation Principles and Practices: A Handbook for Northwest Health Foundation Grantees*. Portland: Northwest Health Foundation. 2000. Permission of the Foundation to use this material is gratefully acknowledged.

## Survey

Examples of surveys are included in the preceding sections for students, faculty, and community.

**What is it?**

- Typically a self-administered questionnaire

- Multiple choice or short answer

- Obtains mostly empirical or quantitative information

- Respondents are selected randomly (e.g., anyone who comes into a certain office on a given day) or it is given to entire population (i.e., all students in a service-learning class)

- If administered to a sample of a larger group, respondents represent the whole population being studied

**Why/when is it used?**

- To assess impact of program, activity, or course

- To assess customer/client satisfaction (e.g., student or community partner satisfaction)

- To compare findings over time or across sites

- To generalize results to a larger population

- To reach a large number of respondents quickly and at low cost

- If general (as compared to individualized) responses are appropriate

**Types of questions**

- Check lists: respondent checks answer(s) that apply to them

- Quality and intensity scales (5 point balanced scales, for example strongly satisfied, satisfied, neutral, dissatisfied, strongly dissatisfied): measure student satisfaction, extent of agreement with statements, quality of service, etc.

- Frequency scales: number of events, activities

- Story identification: offer fictional scenarios and respondent indicates which they relate to (works well with children)

- Ranking: rate preferences (most preferred = 1; next most preferred = 2; etc.)

- Demographics: age group, gender, race, level of education, income, etc.

- Last question: "Do you have any additional comments?"

- Make sure you avoid any "leading" questions that point the respondent toward a particular answer

- Ensure the questions are framed in the language/culture of respondents (such as appropriate literacy level, or level of sophistication of terminology)

## Format

- Introduction: length of time it will take to complete, what the findings will be used for, why the respondent should complete it, why it is important

- Easy opening questions to engage respondent

- Smooth flow of items; questions in logical sequence

- Build up to sensitive questions

- Use transition sentences to clarify the focus of sections of survey (e.g., "These next questions ask about volunteer service you may have done in the past.")

- Skip patterns: make it clear when and how respondents should skip questions that may be irrelevant to them based on responses to previous questions

- Conclusion: where to return survey and by what date; thank you

## The cover letter offers information about the study and about the role of the respondent:

- Purpose, benefit to people

- Who is doing the study, who is paying for it, contact person

- Make the respondent feel important

- Assure confidentiality or anonymity

- Offer opportunity to see study results

- When and how they are to return the survey

- Thank you

- Who to contact if they have questions (and phone number or email)

- Signed letter with original signature; provide name and title of person

### Conducting a survey

- Pre-test the survey on at least ten people before administering it with your population group to troubleshoot some of the following common problems:

  —Confusing wording or use of jargon

  —Uniform meaning of language

  —Appropriate answer choices offered in multiple choice or ranking questions

  —Eliminate double-barreled questions (e.g., "how satisfied are you with your educational program and the number of service-learning courses you have taken?")

- If the evaluator is administering the survey verbally, he/she should read the questions and choice of answers exactly as written and offer little or no clarification or interpretation.

- Note that with some groups (for example, children or the mentally ill), it is better to administer the survey by reading it, but responses are still completed in the same way as if the individual respondent was filling out the survey by themselves.

### Getting the best responses

- Use inviting, colored paper (pale blue, pale yellow if mailing; vibrant colors if at an event where you want the surveys noticed and easily identified)

- Include a self-addressed, stamped return envelope (although you can save money by not stamping the envelope)

- Cover letter that is personal with an original signature (use blue pen to show it is not mass printed)

- Short length of survey

- Promise of confidentiality or anonymity

- Advance notification: let people know they will be receiving the survey and when

- Send by first class mail (although you can save money sending it third class if your organization has non-profit mailing status)

- Incentives (monetary or otherwise)

### What to do with the data (analysis)

- Ensure you have someone on staff who has expertise in statistical analysis, or that you contract with someone with these skills

- Each survey response should be given a unique identification number

- Individual responses should be coded (using numbers) to facilitate analysis; the coding scheme needs to be identical across respondents

- Quantitative data can be analyzed using a computer software package such as Microsoft Excel for simple calculations, or SPSS (Statistical Package for the Social Sciences) for more detailed analysis

- Qualitative responses should be summarized and reviewed to identify any key themes

- Prepare tables (for quantitative data) and narrative (for both quantitative and qualitative) that report the findings according to the indicators and key concepts identified in your assessment matrix

- Descriptive statistics such as frequencies, means, and modes are easily obtained. They are useful to describe characteristics of a group of students or faculty, of partner organizations, or of program utilization.

- Standard deviations are used to assess differences between items (such as responses to a different teaching style, changes in expressed attitudes, or changes in behavior due to interventions).

- Cross-tabulations (or correlations) enable you to look at differences in frequencies by different groups or categories (such as satisfaction with educational programs across different students by major/discipline).

- Chi-square is a useful tool to correlate demographic data among groups (for example by geographic location or by ethnicity/race).

- Factor analysis can reduce items from a long list into categories of items that are closely related and can be used for subsequent analysis. This could involve, for example, condensing a list of several dozen socio-cultural belief statements into a small number of themes that summarize the long list.

- Analysis of Variance (ANOVA) can be useful to explore the existence of variation within and between groups on either single items or on groups of items created through factor analysis. Where there are a large number of respondents, this is a more precise tool to learn the same things as through standard deviations, cross-tabulations, or Chi-square.

# Interview

Interview protocols are provided in the previous sections for students, faculty, community partners, and institutional representatives (both administrators and new faculty).

## What is it?

- Evaluator/researcher meets individually with interviewee (university administrators, partner organization staff or board members, students, faculty) for a one-on-one conversation for about one hour

- A semi-structured means for collecting information

- Obtains mostly qualitative information

- Best conducted by one person with the conversation taped; ideally a second person is present as a note-taker (for back up in case the tape is not audible)

- Attention needs to be given to format and environment to ensure the location is conducive to conversation, non-threatening to the respondent, and establishes a level of comfort between the interviewer and the respondent (therefore be attentive to dress and body language)

## Why/when is it used?

- To assess effectiveness of program or activity

- To assess stakeholder (i.e., students, faculty, partners, etc.) satisfaction with program or activity

- To assess impact of program or activity

- To gain information based on individual perspectives and perceptions

- If individual observations and in-person communication will contribute more to the evaluation

## Format: introduction

- Purpose of study

- Your role in the study

- Participation is considered to be informed consent

- Assure confidentiality

- Anticipated length of interview

- If tape recording, ask permission and explain that the tape is to assist in transcription purposes only
- Clarify any potentially confusing wording, acronyms, or jargon
- Let interviewee know that they can refuse to answer any questions without endangering their relationship with any entity related to the evaluation or program

## Format of questions

- Open ended
- Probe for personal perspective (e.g., "in your own words, tell me…." or "in your opinion…")
- Interview questions and anticipated answers should pertain to personal experience
- Assign approximate time to each question so all questions can be covered in allotted time
- End with "Thank you" and indicate whether a transcript will be provided

## What to do with the data (analysis)

- Transcribe the notes and/or tapes as soon as possible after each interview
- Review the transcripts several times and code for key words and themes
- Organize the key words and themes into patterns, by using colored highlighters to distinguish themes; by cutting and pasting an electronic version; or whatever method works best to help you become familiar with the information
- Compare these patterns to your indicators and key concepts
- Write narrative to reflect your findings

## Focus Group

Focus group protocols are included in the previous sections for students and for community partners. Focus groups could also be conducted with faculty when sufficient faculty have participated in a similar activity; similarly, they could be conducted with institutional administrators if a group discussion offered the most benefit for the data collection for assessment.

### What is it?

- Informal, small group discussion

- Obtains in-depth, qualitative information

- Led by a moderator/facilitator following a predetermined protocol

- Participants are chosen based on some commonality

### Why/when is it used?

- To develop a deeper understanding of a program or activity

- To explore new ideas from the perspectives of a group of key informants

- To provide a forum for issues to arise that have not been considered

- To generate interactive discussion among participants

### Characteristics of a focus group

- Each group is kept small to encourage interaction among participants (6-10 participants)

- Each session usually lasts one hour to one and one half hours

- The conversation is restricted to no more than three to five related topics (e.g., experiences with service-learning, changes in orientation to community work, barriers to service-learning)

- The moderator has a script that outlines the major topics to keep the conversation focused, and does not participate in the dialogue or express any opinions

- Best facilitated by one neutral person with the conversation taped; ideally a second person is present as a note-taker (for back up in case the tape is not audible)

- Attention needs to be given to format and environment to ensure the location where the focus group is conducted is conducive to conversation, non-threatening to the respondents, and establishes a level of comfort between the facilitator and the respondents (therefore be attentive to dress and body language)

**Format: introduction**

- Goal(s) of the focus group: what you want to learn

- How the focus group will work: interactive, conversational, everyone participates, encourage getting all ideas stated, not necessary to reach agreement, no right or wrong answer

- Role of moderator (facilitating, not discussing)

- Let participants know that the session will be tape recorded and for what the tape will be used; indicate that transcript will have no names in it and will be seen only by evaluators

- Ensure confidentiality

- Request that participants speak loudly, clearly, and one at a time

**Format: questions**

- Narrowly defined questions keep the conversation focused

- Questions are often very similar to those used in an interview, with the recognition that a group will be answering rather than one person

- Easy opening question to engage participants

- Questions should become increasingly specific as the discussion proceeds

- Include optional follow-up or probing questions in the protocol to help the facilitator to elicit the desired information

- Assign an approximate time frame to each question so that all topics are covered

- Final question: "Are there any other comments you'd like to share?"

- End with "Thank you" and indicate whether a transcript will be provided

**Focus group participants**

- Determine whose perspective you want (student participants, faculty, community partner organization administrators, partner board members, university administrators, other stakeholders)

- Different target populations should not be invited to the same session, as they may inhibit or skew each other's comments

- Participants are often recruited from class rosters, faculty lists, partner lists, or other databases

- Use a screening questionnaire if you need to know more about potential participants before making selection

### Conducting a focus group

- Be flexible with the sequence of questions. If participants bring up an issue early that comes later in the list of questions, let the conversation happen naturally (with minimal guidance).

- Select a facilitator carefully so that they are someone whose demographics will not bias participants' responses.

- An in-house staff person (university administrator, graduate student, faculty with assessment expertise) has more inside knowledge of programs, but may have less experience, and may introduce a level of bias if they are the facilitator.

- A professional moderator may be expensive, but has more experience and has an emotional distance that allows for greater objectivity. In universities there are often many individuals with experience facilitating focus groups who will donate their time.

- Communicate very clearly to the facilitator (particularly if using an outside professional) a description of the program or ideas being explored, and what your needs are. This way, s/he will know when to follow up and when to ignore unexpected comments.

- Schedule the focus group at a time that is generally convenient for your participants.

### What to do with the data (analysis)

- Transcribe the tapes and notes from a focus group as soon as possible after the session. Remember that focus groups generate a large body of rich, textual data.

- Analyze the notes by organizing the data into meaningful subsections — either around the questions posed or around the key concepts reflected by the questions.

- Code the data by identifying meaningful phrases and quotes.

- Organize the key words and themes into patterns, by using colored highlighters to distinguish themes; by cutting and pasting an electronic version; or whatever method works best to help you become familiar with the information.

- Search for patterns within and across subsections.

- Compare these patterns to your indicators and key concepts.

- Write narrative to reflect your findings.

# Observation

A number of methods are provided in the faculty section for classroom observation. Observation protocols are also included for community and institutional observations.

## What is it?

- Systematic technique using one's eyes, ears and other senses

- Uses a standardized grading or ranking to produce quantitative and qualitative information

- Uses "trained observers"

## Why/when is it used?

- To assess aspects of programs or activities that require looking at or listening to the activity in process. Some examples one might observe are:

  —Provision of service by students at community partner organization

  —Dynamics of interaction between faculty and students in classroom setting

  —Interactions of community partners, agency clients and students

  —Content of, and interactions at, community advisory board meetings at the university

- To gain additional insights about a program (or whatever is being evaluated) by direct observation of activities, interactions, events, etc.

## Characteristics of observation

- Uses trained observers to assure accuracy across observers and over time

- Precise rating scales used with specific attributes for each score/grade

- If using rating scales, scales should be no less than three and no more than seven levels

- Potentially difficult distinctions should be noted

- Use an observer protocol form to guide recording of observation

- Those being observed do not know what the observer is measuring (they are unaware of content of protocol)

### What to do with the data (analysis)

- Review the observation protocol and notes as soon as possible after the observation.

- Analyze the notes by organizing the data into meaningful subsections — either around the questions posed or around the key concepts reflected by the questions.

- Organize the key words and themes into patterns, by using colored highlighters to distinguish themes; by cutting and pasting an electronic version; or whatever method works best to help you become familiar with the information.

- Search for patterns within and across subsections

- Compare these patterns to other findings for the indicators and key concepts

- Write brief narrative to reflect your findings, and integrate this narrative into your overall report.

## Documentation

Several examples of documentation review for faculty are provided, including a syllabus analysis and a curriculum vitae analysis. A description of documentation review for institutional assessment is also included.

### What is it?

- Use of various kinds of existing narrative or other data

- Information is not collected first-hand but is available for review and analysis ("secondary" data)

- Narrative data may include program or partner organization records, policies, procedures, minutes, program descriptions, syllabi, curricula vitae, faculty journals, etc.

- Use of existing reports such as budgetary information, grant history, service provision or utilization reports, faculty or partner profiles, etc.

### Why/when is it used?

- To gather historical information

- To assess the processes involved in delivering or supporting the service-learning course

- To augment interpretation of primary data through records of other activities relevant to the assessment

**Types of information frequently looked for in university records**

- Information on student, faculty, partner or course characteristics

- Number and nature of service-learning courses

- Success of work (e.g., number of grants funded related to service-learning; number of faculty scholarly presentations or publications related to their experiences with service-learning)

- Administrative/organizational information that may set context for interpretation of other data

**Potential problems and ways to alleviate them**

MISSING OR INCOMPLETE DATA

- Go back to the data and related sources (such as by interviewing faculty) to fill in as many gaps as possible (do not redo documents but do augment the assessment data collection)

- Determine whether part or all of the assessment needs to be modified because of a lack of key information

- Exclude missing data or provide a "best estimate" of the missing values

DATA AVAILABLE ONLY IN SIMPLIFIED, OVERLY AGGREGATED FORM  (e.g., number of students involved, but not by course, discipline or major, or demographic descriptors)

- Where feasible, go back into the records to reconstruct the needed data

- Conduct new, original data collection

- Drop the unavailable disaggregated data from the evaluation

UNKNOWN, DIFFERENT, OR CHANGING DEFINITIONS OF DATA ELEMENTS (e.g., measuring the academic performance of students, when requirements for entering GPA changed from 2.75 to 3.00)

- Make feasible adjustments to make data more comparable

- Focus on percentage changes rather than absolute values

- Drop analysis of such data elements when the problem is insurmountable

DATA THAT ARE LINKED ACROSS TIME AND COURSES / PROGRAMS (e.g., program "A" in your university tracks students by year of admission to university; program "B" tracks by declared major)

- Be sure that the outcome data apply to the particular individuals or work elements addressed by the evaluation

- Track individuals/work elements between courses/programs using such identifiers as social security numbers

- Look for variations in spellings, nicknames, aliases, etc. (many "smart" computer programs can now do this for you)

- Determine whether such individual data is really necessary, or whether aggregated data (e.g., by course) is sufficient

**CONFIDENTIALITY AND PRIVACY CONSIDERATIONS**

- Secure needed permissions from persons about whom individual data are needed

- Avoid recording individual names; instead use code identifiers

- Secure any lists that link code identifiers to individual names. Destroy these after the evaluation requirements are met

- Obtain data without identifiers from source organizations

- Be sure to go through human subjects review (or equivalent) if appropriate

## What to do with the data (analysis)

- Develop a framework based on your indicators and key concepts in which you can record key findings from the documentation (sometimes creating a table or a blank matrix is useful). This helps to guide your thinking as you review the various documents and will keep you focused on your key indicators and concepts.

- Search for patterns in those findings that reflect the indicators and key concepts.

- Compare these patterns to other findings for the indicators and key concepts.

- Write brief narrative to reflect your findings, and integrate this narrative into your overall report.

## Critical Incident Report

An example of a critical incident report is included in the institutional section, with a focus on program administrators. Critical incident reports could also be used by students (as a form of reflection) or faculty.

**What is it?**

- A reflective document requested of individuals involved in the program for purposes of evaluation

- A look back at major events (anticipated or unanticipated) that affected the program in positive or negative ways

- Documentation of key events that, in retrospect, significantly accelerated work towards accomplishment of goals; OR created barriers to goal accomplishment; OR enabled the organization to overcome barriers

**Why/when is it used?**

- To provide an overview of how program development issues affect outcomes

- To document the processes involved in program administration from a broad perspective over time (rather than a daily log)

**Characteristics of critical incident reports**

- List of critical incidents in chronological order with dates provided and description of why the event is viewed as "critical"

- Examples of critical incidents are: relevant institutional policy on service-learning adopted, grant awarded (or not awarded), key staff member hired or terminated, physical relocation of offices, new faculty promotion and tenure criteria adopted, accreditation report received, etc.

**What to do with the data (analysis)**

- Develop a framework based on your indicators and key concepts in which you can record key findings from the critical incident reports (sometimes creating a table or a blank matrix is useful). This helps to guide your thinking as you review the various documents and will keep you focused on your key indicators and concepts.

- Search for patterns in those findings that reflect the indicators and key concepts

- Compare these patterns to other findings for the indicators and key concepts

- Write brief narrative to reflect your findings, and integrate this narrative into your overall report

# Journal

A journal protocol is provided in the faculty section. Note that student journals are not included here, as they are usually intended primarily as a learning strategy in service-learning courses; as faculty journals are presented here, they are intended as a reflective tool to gain insights about the process and activities of offering service-learning courses.

## What is it?

- Personal reflections and observations by individuals; recorded on a regular basis

- Provides information related to the program being assessed from a personal perspective of key individuals involved in the program

## Why/when is it used?

- To assess subtle changes in the program or individual reporting over time

- To encourage key individuals to reflect upon events and assess both their personal reactions and the organization's responses

## Characteristics of a journal

- Personal perspective

- Highly reflective

- Daily/weekly observations about program occurrences, student or community activities, etc. and responses

- Free-form or in response to general guided questions

## What to do with the data (analysis)

- Develop a framework based on your indicators and key concepts in which you can record key findings from the journals (sometimes creating a table or a blank matrix is useful). This helps to guide your thinking as you review the various documents and will keep you focused on your key indicators and concepts.

- Collect the journals periodically (if over a long-term period) or once at the end of a pre-scribed period of time. For faculty keeping a journal during a course, you may wish to collect the journals approximately half-way through the course session to get a sense of the observations, and then again immediately following the end of the course.

- Read each journal, and analyze the content using the framework you have developed.

- Search for patterns in those findings that reflect the indicators and key concepts. Record or track these by using colored highlighters to distinguish themes; by cutting and pasting an electronic version of the journals; or by whatever method works best to help you become familiar with the information.

- Compare these patterns to other findings for the indicators and key concepts.

- Write brief narrative to reflect your findings, and integrate this narrative into your overall report.

# References

Alt, M.A. & E.A. Medrich. (1994). "Student Outcomes from Participation in Community Service." Paper prepared for the U.S. Department of Education Office of Research.

Anderson, S.M. (1998). "Service-learning: A National Strategy for Youth Development." Position paper for Education Policy Task force, Institute for Communication Policy Studies, George Washington University.

Annie E. Casey Foundation. (1999). "Research and Evaluation at the Annie E. Casey Foundation." [available at http://www.aecf.org]

Astin, A. (1993). *Assessment for Excellence.* Phoenix: Oryx Press.

Astin, A., & Gamson, Z. (1983). "Academic Workplace: New Demands, Heightened Tensions." ASHE-ERIC Higher Education Research Report No. 10. Washington, DC: Association for the Study of Higher Education.

Astin, A.W. & L. Sax. (1998). "How Undergraduates Are Affected by Service Participation." *Journal of College Student Development* 39 (3): 251–263.

Astin, A., L Vogelgesang, E. Ikeda, & J. Yee. (2000). "How Service-learning Affects Students." Los Angeles: University of California, Los Angeles, Higher Education Research Institute.

Barr, Robert B. & John Tagg. (1995). "From Teaching to Learning: A New Paradigm for Undergraduate Education." *Change* 27 (November/December): 13–25.

Batchelder, T., & S. Root. (1999). "Effects of an Undergraduate Program to Integrate Academic Learning and Service: Cognitive, Prosocial Cognitive, and Identity Outcomes." In M.C. Sullivan, R.A. Myers, C.D. Bradfield, & D.L. Street (Eds.). *Service-learning: Educating Students for Life.* Harrisonburg, VA: James Madison University.

Battistoni, R. M. (1997). Service-Learning as Civic Learning: Lessons We Can Learn from Our Students. In G. Reeher & J. Cammarano (Eds.). *Education for Citizenship*, p. 31–49. Lanham, MD: Rowman and Littlefield Publishers.

Berson, J.S. and W.F. Youkin. (1998). "Doing Well by Doing Good: A Study of the Effects of a Service-Learning Experience on Student Success." Paper presented at the annual meeting of the American Society of Higher Education, Miami, FL.

Bess, J. (1982). *New Directions for Teaching and Learning: Motivating Professors to Teach Effectively*. San Francisco: Jossey-Bass Inc., Publishers.

Bringle, R., & Hatcher, J. (1995). "A Service-learning Curriculum for Faculty." *Michigan Journal of Community Service Learning* 2: 114-122.

Bringle, Robert, & Hatcher, Julie (1998). "Implementing Service Learning in Higher Education." *Journal of Research and Development in Education* 29 (4): 31-41.

Bringle, R.G. & Hatcher, J.A. (2000). "Institutionalization of Service Learning in Higher Education." *The Journal of Higher Education* 71 (3): 273-290.

Brookfield, Stephen D. (1995). *Becoming a Critically Reflective Teacher*. San Francisco: Jossey-Bass Inc., Publishers.

Bucco, D.A. & Busch, J.A. (1996). "Starting a Service-Learning Program." In B. Jacoby & Associates (Eds.). *Service Learning in Higher Education*, p. 231-245). San Francisco: Jossey-Bass Publishers.

Buchanan, R. (1997). "Service-learning Survey Results." Unpublished manuscript, University of Utah, Bennion Community Service Center, Salt Lake City.

Campus Compact. (1999). *Presidents' Fourth of July Declaration on the Civic Responsibility of Higher Education*. Providence, RI: Campus Compact. [Also available at http://www.compact.org]

Campus Compact. (2000). *Introduction to Service-Learning Toolkit: Readings and Resources for Faculty*. Providence, RI: Campus Compact.

Clarke, M. (2000). *Evaluating the Community Impact of Service-learning: The 3-I Model*. Unpublished doctoral dissertation. Nashville: Peabody College of Vanderbilt University.

Connell, J., A. Kubisch, L. Schorr, & C. Weiss (eds.). (1995). *New Approaches to Evaluating Community Initiatives: Concepts, Methods and Contexts*. Washington, DC: The Aspen Institute.

Creswell, J.W. (1994). *Qualitative and Quantitative Approaches.* Thousand Oaks, CA: Sage Publications.

Cruz, N.I. & D.E. Giles. (2000). "Where's the Community in Service-learning Research?" *Michigan Journal of Community Service Learning* Special Issue on Strategic Directions for Service Learning Research (Fall): 28-34.

Deci, E., & Ryan, R. (1982). "Intrinsic Motivation to Teach: Possibilities and Obstacles in Our Colleges and Universities." In J. Bess, ed. *New Directions for Teaching and Learning: Motivating Professors to Teach Effectively.* San Francisco: Jossey-Bass Inc., Publishers.

Denzin, Norman K. and Yvonna S. Lincoln, eds. (1998a). *Collecting and Interpreting Qualitative Materials.* Thousand Oaks, CA: Sage Publications, Inc.

Denzin, Norman K. and Yvonna S. Lincoln, eds. (1998b). *Strategies of Qualitative Inquiry.* Thousand Oaks, CA: Sage Publications, Inc.

Dillman, Don A. (1999). *Mail and Internet Surveys: The Tailored Design Method.* 2nd ed. New York: Free Press.

Driscoll, Amy. (2000). "Studying Faculty and Service-learning: Directions for Inquiry and Development." *Michigan Journal of Community Service Learning* Special Issue on Strategic Directions for Service Learning Research (Fall): 35-41.

Driscoll, Amy, Sherril B. Gelmon, Barbara A. Holland, Seanna Kerrigan, M.J. Longley, & Amy Spring. (1997). *Assessing the Impact of Service Learning: A Workbook of Strategies and Methods.* 1st edition. Portland: Center for Academic Excellence, Portland State University.

Driscoll, Amy, Sherril B. Gelmon, Barbara A. Holland, Seanna Kerrigan, Amy Spring, Kari Grosvold, & M.J. Longley. (1998). *Assessing the Impact of Service Learning: A Workbook of Strategies and Methods.* 2nd edition. Portland: Portland State University, Center for Academic Excellence.

Driscoll, Amy, Barbara A. Holland, Sherril B. Gelmon, & Seanna Kerrigan. (1996). "An Assessment Model for Service Learning: Comprehensive Case Studies of Impact on Faculty, Students, Community and Institution." *Michigan Journal of Community Service Learning* 3 (Fall): 66–71.

Driscoll, Amy & Ernest Lynton. (1999). *Making Outreach Visible: A Guide to Documenting Professional Service and Outreach.* Washington DC: American Association for Higher Education.

Driscoll, Amy, Joan Strouse & M.J. Longley. (1997). "Changing Roles for Community, Students, and Faculty in Community-Based Learning Courses." *Journal of Higher Education and Lifelong Learning* 33–45.

Ehrlich, Thomas. (2000). *Civic Responsibility and Higher Education*. Phoenix: American Council on Education and Oryx Press.

Eyler, J. (2000). "What Do We Most Need To Know about the Impact of Service-Learning on Student Learning?" *Michigan Journal of Community Service-Learning* Special Issue on Strategic Directions for Service Learning Research (Fall): 11–17.

Eyler, J., & D.E. Giles. (1994). "The Impact of a College Community Service Laboratory on Students' Personal, Social, and Cognitive Outcomes." *Journal of Adolescence* 17: 327-339.

Eyler, J., & D.E. Giles. (1999). *Where's the Learning in Service-Learning?* San Francisco, CA: Jossey-Bass Inc., Publishers.

Eyler, J., D.E. Giles, & C. Gray. (1999). "At a Glance: Summary and Annotated Bibliography of Recent Service-Learning Research in Higher Education." Minneapolis, MN: Learn & Serve America National Service-Learning Clearinghouse.

Fink, Arlene, ed. (1995). *The Survey Kit*. Thousand Oaks, CA: Sage Publications, Inc. Includes 9 volumes (available individually or as a set):

Vol. 1: The Survey Handbook (Arlene Fink).

Vol. 2: How to Ask Survey Questions (Arlene Fink).

Vol. 3: How to Conduct Self-Administered Mail Surveys (Linda Bourque and Eve Fielder).

Vol. 4: How to Conduct Interviews by Telephone and in Person (James Frey and Sabine Mertens Oishi).

Vol. 5: How to Design Surveys (Arlene Fink).

Vol. 6: How to Sample in Surveys (Arlene Fink).

Vol. 7: How to Measure Survey Reliability and Validity (Mark Litwin).

Vol. 8: How to Analyze Survey Data (Arlene Fink).

Vol. 9: How to Report on Surveys (Arlene Fink).

Furco, Andrew. (2000). "Self-Assessment Rubric for the Institutionalization of Service-Learning in Higher Education." Berkeley: University of California at Berkeley.

Gelmon, Sherril B. (1997). "Intentional Improvement: The Deliberate Linkage of Assessment and Accreditation." In *Assessing Impact: Evidence and Action*. Washington, DC: American Association of Higher Education, p. 51–65.

Gelmon, Sherril B. (2000a). "Challenges in Assessing Service-learning." *Michigan Journal of Community Service Learning* Special Issue on Strategic Directions for Service Learning Research (Fall): 84–90.

Gelmon, Sherril B. (2000b). "How Do We Know That Our Work Makes A Difference? Assessment Strategies for Service-Learning and Civic Engagement." *Metropolitan Universities* 11 (Fall): 28–39.

Gelmon, Sherril B. & Lisa Barnett, with the CBQIE-HP Technical Assistant Team. (1998). *Community-Based Quality Improvement in Education for the Health Professions: Evaluation Report, 1997–1998*. Portland: Portland State University.

Gelmon, Sherril B. & Amy Connell. (2000). *Program Evaluation Principles and Practices: A Handbook for Northwest Health Foundation Grantees*. Portland: Northwest Health Foundation.

Gelmon, Sherril B., Barbara A. Holland & Anu F. Shinnamon. (1998). *Health Professions Schools in Service to the Nation: 1996–1998 Final Evaluation Report*. San Francisco: Community-Campus Partnerships for Health, UCSF Center for the Health Professions. [available from http://futurehealth.ucsf.edu/ccph.htm]

Gelmon, Sherril B., Barbara A. Holland, Anu F. Shinnamon & Beth A. Morris. (1998). "Community-Based Education and Service: The HPSISN Experience." *Journal of Interprofessional Care* 12 (#3): 257–272.

Gelmon, Sherril B., Barbara A. Holland, Sarena D. Seifer, Anu F. Shnnamon, & Kara Connors. (1998). "Community-University Partnerships for Mutual Learning." *Michigan Journal of Community Service Learning* 5 (Fall): 97-107.

Gelmon, Sherril B., Leslie G. McBride, Sharon Hill, Leslie Chester, & Jessica Guernsey. (1998). *Evaluation of the Portland Health Communities Initiative 1996–1998*. Portland: Healthy Communities and Portland State University.

Gelmon, Sherril B., Andrea W. White, Letitia Carlson, & Linda Norman. (2000). "Making Organizational Change to Achieve Improvement and Interprofessional Learning: Perspectives from Health Professions Educators." *Journal of Interprofessional Care* 14 (No. 2): 131–146.

Giles, D.E., & J. Eyler. (1994). "The Theoretical Roots of Service-Learning in John Dewey: Toward a Theory of Service-Learning." *Michigan Journal of Community Service-Learning* 1: 77--5.

Giles, Dwight E., Ellen Porter Honnet, & Sally Migliore, eds.. (1991). "Research Agenda for Combining Service and Learning in the 1990s." Raleigh, NC: National Society of Internships and Experiential Education.

Gilbert, M.K., C. Holdt, C. & K. Christopherson. (1998). "Letting Feminist Knowledge Serve the City." In M. Mayberry & E. Rose (Eds.). *Meeting the Challenge: Innovative Feminist Pedagogies in Action,* p. 319–339. Newbury Park, CA: Sage Publishers.

Gray, M.J., E.H. Ondaatje, S. Geschwind, R. Fricker, C. Goldman, T. Kaganoff, A. Robyn, M. Sundt, L. Vogelsang, & S. Klein. (1999). *Combining Service and Learning in Higher Education.* Santa Monica, CA: Rand Corporation.

Hammond, C. (1994). "Faculty Motivation and Satisfaction in Michigan Higher Education." *Michigan Journal of Community Service Learning* 1 (Fall): 42-49.

Harkavy, I., J. Puckett, & D. Romer. (2000). "Action Research: Bridging Service and Research." *Michigan Journal of Community Service Learning* Special Issue on Strategic Directions for Service Learning Research (Fall): 113-118.

Holland, Barbara A. (1997). "Analyzing Institutional Commitment to Service: A Model of Key Organizational Factors." *Michigan Journal of Community Service Learning.* 4:30-41.

Holland, Barbara A. (1999a). "Factors and Strategies that Influence Faculty Involvement in Service." *Journal of Public Service and Outreach.* 4 (1): 37-44.

Holland, Barbara A. (1999b). "Implementing Urban Missions Project: 1998-99 Evaluation Report." Washington, DC: Council of Independent Colleges.

Holland, Barbara A. (2000a). "Evaluation Plan for the PSU Masters in Tribal Administration Program." Unpublished report, Portland State University.

Holland, Barbara A. (2000b). "The Engaged Institution and Sustainable Partnerships: Key Characteristics and Effective Change Strategies." Presented at HUD Regional Conference, San Diego, December 2000.

Holland, Barbara A. (2001, forthcoming). "A Comprehensive Model for Assessing Service-Learning and Community-University Partnerships." In Mark Canada and Bruce Speck, eds. *Service Learning: Practical Advice and Models*. San Francisco: Jossey-Bass, Inc., Publishers.

Holland, Barbara A. (2001, forthcoming). "Implementing Urban Missions Project: An Overview of Lessons Learned." *Metropolitan Universities* 12 (3).

Holland, Barbara A. & Sherril B. Gelmon. (1998). "The State of the "Engaged Campus": What Have We Learned About Building and Sustaining University-Community Partnerships?" *AAHE Bulletin* 51 (October): 3–6.

Hollander, Elizabeth & Matthew Hartley. (2000). "Civic Renewal in Higher Education: The State of the Movement and the Need for a National Network." In Thomas Ehrlich, ed. *Civic Responsibility and Higher Education*, p. 345–366. Phoenix: American Council on Education and Oryx Press.

Honnet, E.P. & S. Poulsen. (1989). "Principles of Good Practice in Combining Service and Learning." Wingspread Special Report. Racine, WI: Johnson Foundation.

Howard, Jeffrey P. (1995). Unpublished materials. Ann Arbor: University of Michigan.

Johnson, D.B. (1996). "Implementing a College-Wide Service Learning Initiative: The Faculty Coordinator's Role." *Expanding Boundaries: Serving and Learning*. Washington DC: Corporation for National Service.

Jordan, K.L. (1994). "The Relationship of Service-Learning and College Student Development." Unpublished doctoral dissertation. Blacksburg, VA: Virginia Polytechnic Institute and State University.

Keith, N.Z. (1998). "Community Service for Community-Building: The School-based Service Corps as Border Crossers." *Michigan Journal of Community Service Learning* 5 (Fall): 86–98.

Kellogg Commission on the Future of State and Land-Grant Institutions. (1999). *Returning to Our Roots: The Engaged Institution*. Washington, D.C.: National Association of State Universities and Land-Grant Colleges.

Knapp, Marian L., Nancy M. Bennett, James D. Plumb, & Jamie L. Robinson. (2000). "Community-based Quality Improvement Education for the Health Professions: Balancing Benefits for Communities and Students." *Journal of Interprofessional Care* 14 (2): 119-130.

Kretzman, John & John McKnight. (1993) *Building Communities from the Inside Out: A Path Toward Finding and Mobilizing a Community's Assets*. Chicago, IL: ACTA Publications.

Langley, Gerald J., Kevin M. Nolan, Thomas W. Nolan, Clifford L. Norman, & Lloyd P. Provost. (1996). *The Improvement Guide*. San Francisco: Jossey-Bass Inc., Publishers.

Lynton, E. (1995). *Making the Case for Professional Service*. Washington, DC: American Association for Higher Education.

Magruder, Jack, Michael A. McManis, & Candace C. Young. (1997). "The Right Idea at the Right Time: Development of a Transformational Assessment Culture." In Peter J. Gray & Trudy W. Banta, eds. *The Campus-Level Impact of Assessment: Progress, Problems, and Possibilities. New Directions for Higher Education* 100 (Winter): 17–29. San Francisco: Jossey-Bass Inc., Publishers.

McKeachie, W. (1982). "The Rewards of Teaching." In J. Bess, ed. *New Directions for Teaching and Learning: Motivating Professors to Teach Effectively*. San Francisco: Jossey-Bass Inc., Publishers.

Miles, M.B. & A.M. Huberman. (1994). *Qualitative Data Analysis*. Thousand Oaks: Sage Publications.

Morgan, David L. (1993). *Successful Focus Groups*. Newbury Park, CA: Sage Publications, Inc.

Morgan, David L. (1997). *Focus Groups as Qualitative Research*. Newbury Park, CA: Sage Publications, Inc.

Morgan, David L. (1998). *The Focus Group Guidebook*. Thousand Oaks: Sage Publications.

Myers-Lipton, S.J. (1996). "Effect of a Comprehensive Service-Learning Program on College Students Level of Modern Racism." *Michigan Journal of Community Service-Learning* 3 (1): 44–54.

Palomba, Catherine A. (1997). "Assessment at Ball State University." In Peter J. Gray & Trudy W. Banta, eds. *The Campus-Level Impact of Assessment: Progress, Problems, and Possibilities. New Directions for Higher Education* 100 (Winter): 31–45. San Francisco: Jossey-Bass Inc., Publishers.

Patton, Michael Quinn. (1997). *Utilization Focused Evaluation: The New Century Edition.* Thousand Oaks, CA: Sage Publications, Inc.

Petersen, A. (1998). *W.K. Kellogg Foundation Evaluation Handbook.* Battle Creek, MI: W.K. Kellogg Foundation.

Peterson, Robert A. (2000). *Constructing Effective Questionnaires.* Thousand Oaks, CA: Sage Publications, Inc.

Ramaley, Judith. (1996). Personal communication. Portland: Portland State University.

Rice, D., & Stacey, K. (1997). "Small Group Dynamics as a Catalyst for Change: A Faculty Development Model for Academic Service-Learning." *Michigan Journal of Community Service Learning* 4 (Fall): 57–64.

Rubin, S. (1996). "Institutionalizing Service-learning." In B. Jacoby & Associates (Eds.), *Service Learning in Higher Education,* p. 297–316. San Francisco: Jossey-Bass Publishers.

Sax, L., & A. Astin. (1996). "The Impact of College on Post College Involvement in Volunteerism and Community Service." Paper presented at the annual meeting of the Association for Institutional Research, Albuquerque, NM.

Scholtes, Peter R. (1997). "Communities as Systems." *Quality Progress* 30: 49-53.

Seifer, Sarena D. & Cheryl A. Maurana. (2000). "Developing and Sustaining Community-Campus Partnerships: Putting Principles Into Practice." *Partnership Perspectives* 1 (Summer): 7–11.

Shinnamon, Anu F., Sherril B. Gelmon, & Barbara A. Holland. (1999). *Methods and Strategies for Assessing Service Learning in the Health Professions.* San Francisco: Community-Campus Partnerships for Health, UCSF Center for the Health Professions. [available from http://future-health.ucsf.edu/ccph.htm]

Sigmon, Robert. (1979). "Service-learning: Three Principles." *Synergist* 8: 9–11.

Stanton, T. (1990). "Integrating Public Service with Academic Study: The Faculty Role." Providence, RI: Campus Compact.

Stanton, Timothy. (1994). "The Experience of Faculty Participants in Instructional Development Seminar on Service-Learning." *Michigan Journal of Community Service Learning* 1: 7–20.

Strauss, Anselm and J. Corbin. (1990). *Basics of Qualitative Research: Grounded Theory Procedures and Techniques.* Newbury Park, CA: Sage Publications, Inc.

Ward, Kelly. (1996). "Service-learning and Student Volunteerism: Reflections on Institutional Commitment." *Michigan Journal of Community Service Learning* 3:55-65.

Warwick, Donald P. and Charles A. Lininger. (1975). *The Sample Survey: Theory and Practice.* New York: McGraw-Hill, Inc.

Wealthall, S., J. Graham, & C. Turner. (1998). "Building, Maintaining and Repairing the Community-Campus Bridge: Five Years' Experience of Community Groups Educating Medical Students." *Journal of Interprofessional Care* 12 (August): 289-302.

Wechsler, A. & J. Fogel. (1995). "The Outcomes of a Service-Learning Program." *National Society for Experiential Education Quarterly* 21(4): 6-7, 25-26.

Wholey, Joseph S., Harry P. Hatry and Katherine E. Newcomer, eds. (1994). *Handbook of Practical Program Evaluation.* San Francisco: Jossey-Bass Inc., Publishers.

Zlotkowski, Edward. (1999a). "Pedagogy and Engagement." In R. Bringle, R. Games, & E.A. Malloy (eds.). *Colleges and Universities as Citizens,* p. 66–120. Boston: Allyn & Bacon.

Zlotkowski, Edward. (1999b). "A Service-Learning Approach to Faculty Development." In J.P. Howard and R. Rhodes, eds. *Service Learning Pedagogy and Research.* San Francisco: Jossey-Bass Inc., Publishers.

Zlotkowski, Edward. (2000). "Service-Learning Research in the Disciplines." *Michigan Journal of Community Service Learning* Special Issue on Strategic Directions for Service Learning Research (Fall): 61-67.